단기간에 마무리하는 8가지 핵심 비법

비법 담은 중학 영문법

특강편 1

비법 담은 중학 영문법 특강편 1

지은이	한길연, 이나영, 박영은
펴낸이	최희영
책임편집	김종원, 이승혜
감수	오승희, 이지애, 김주희, 이수진, 정은숙
영문교열	David Charlton
디자인	디자인플러스
펴낸곳	(주)웅진컴퍼스
등록번호	제22-2943호
등록일자	2006년 6월 16일
주소	서울특별시 서초구 강남대로39길 15-10 한라비발디스튜디오193 3층
전화	(02)3471-0096
홈페이지	http://www.wjcompass.com
ISBN	979-11-6237-000-1

13 12 11 10 9
24

Photo Credits

All photos © Shutterstock, Inc.

Printed in Korea

CONTENTS

이 책의 구성과 특징

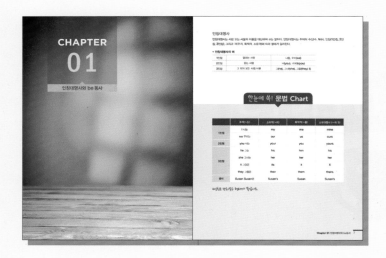

챕터 가이드

각 챕터의 학습 목표, 배울 내용과 함께 중요한 문법의 개념과 용어를 한눈에 보기 쉽도록 정리하였습니다.

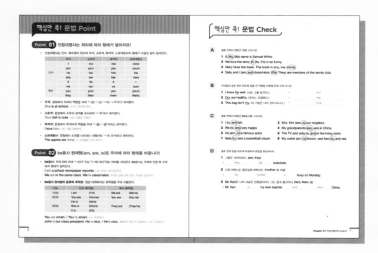

핵심만 쏙! 문법 Point

쉽고 정확한 문법 설명과 최신 교과서의 구문을 반영한 실용적인 예문을 제공합니다.

핵심만 콕! 문법 Check

앞서 배운 문법을 다양한 유형의 문제로 풀어보며 다시 한번 확인하도록 합니다.

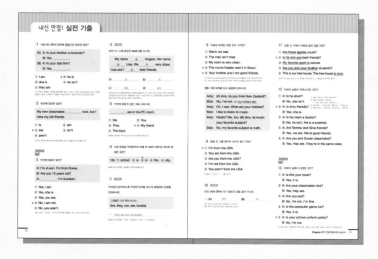

내신 만점! 실전 기출

최근 7년 전국 중학교 기출문제를 최다 빈출 문항 위주로 제공합니다. 또한 비중이 커진 수행평가를 위한 서술형 문제와 고난도 문항까지 완벽 대비합니다.

목차

CHAPTER

01

일반동사

일반동사

be동사와 조동사를 제외한 나머지 모든 동사를 가리켜 일반동사라고 한다. '먹다, 자다, 공부하다, 놀다' 처럼 주어의 동작이나 상태를 나타내는 동사가 모두 일반동사이다. 일반동사도 주어의 인칭, 수에 따라, 그리고 언제의 일을 나타내느냐에 따라 형태가 바뀐다.

• be동사, 일반동사, 조동사

be동사	am, are, is
일반동사	go (가다), come (오다), study (공부하다), like (좋아하다), want (원하다) 등
조동사	can (~할 수 있다), will (~할 것이다), may (~해도 좋다) 등

한눈에 쏙! 문법 Chart

일반동사 현재시제의 문장형태

평서문의 동사형	주어가 1, 2인칭 단수와 모든 복수형 → 동사는 원형으로 쓴다.
	3인칭 단수 → 동사에 (e)s를 붙인다.
부정문	일반적으로 「don't + 동사원형」
	주어가 3인칭 단수일 때 「doesn't + 동사원형」
의문문	일반적으로 「Do + 주어 + 동사원형~?」
	주어가 3인칭 단수일 때 「Does + 주어 + 동사원형~?」

핵심만 쏙! 문법 Point

Point 01 일반동사의 현재형은 인칭과 수에 따라 형태가 달라져요!

- 일반동사는 be동사와 조동사 이외의 동사이다. 일반동사의 현재형은 현재 사실이나 반복되는 습관을 나타낸다.

- 주어가 1인칭, 2인칭이면 단수, 복수 상관없이 동사원형을 쓴다. 3인칭 복수 주어이면, 동사원형을 쓴다.
  I like soccer a lot. 나는 축구를 매우 좋아한다.
  We go to the school music club every Wednesday. 우리는 수요일마다 학교 음악 동아리에 간다.
  You sing very well. 너는 노래를 매우 잘 하는구나.
  They make pizza in the kitchen. 그들은 부엌에서 피자를 만든다.

- 주어가 3인칭 단수일 때 일반동사 현재형은 대개 「동사원형 + -(e)s」의 형태로 쓴다.
  She lives in an apartment. 그녀는 아파트에 산다.
  She goes to school by bus. 그녀는 버스를 타고 학교에 간다.

Point 02 주어가 3인칭 단수이면 일반동사의 현재형은 동사에 –(e)s를 붙여요!

- 주어가 3인칭 단수일 때 일반동사의 현재형 만드는 법

대부분의 일반동사 → 동사원형 + -s	comes, drives, likes, makes, reads, sees, wants
-o, -s, -ch, -sh, -x로 끝나는 동사 → 동사원형 + -es	do**es**, go**es**, pas**ses**, tea**ches**, wa**shes**, fi**xes**, mi**xes**
「자음 + y」로 끝나는 동사 → y를 i로 바꾸고 + -es	cry → cries, fly → flies, study → studies, try → tries, marry → marries, copy → copies
「모음 + y」로 끝나는 동사 → 동사원형 + -s	plays, says, stays
불규칙 변화	have → has

My mom likes flowers. 나의 엄마는 꽃을 좋아한다.
She washes dishes after dinner. 그녀는 저녁 식사 후에 설거지를 한다.
Jane studies very hard for her exam. Jane은 시험을 위해 열심히 공부한다.
Tom plays basketball after school. Tom은 방과 후에 농구를 한다.

핵심만 콕! 문법 Check

A 괄호 안에서 알맞은 말을 고르시오.

1 I (like, likes) reading magazines.
2 You (look, looks) wonderful.
3 My grandmother (write, writes) books for children.
4 The teacher (teach, teaches) social science.
5 Lily and Jaemin (live, lives) in the same apartment building.

B 밑줄 친 부분을 어법에 맞게 고쳐 쓰시오.

1 You <u>plays</u> the violin well.   → _____
2 The student <u>write</u> an essay for homework.   → _____
3 David <u>have</u> many friends.   → _____
4 Tom <u>studys</u> with me after school.   → _____
5 Jane <u>gos</u> swimming on Saturdays.   → _____

C 괄호 안의 동사를 활용하여 문장을 완성하시오. (단, 시제는 현재)

1 Bill _____ an iguana as a pet. (want)
2 You _____ to school very early. (come)
3 Mom _____ coffee in the morning. (drink)
4 The players _____ all the rules of the game. (know)
5 Andy _____ beautiful blue eyes. (have)

D 괄호 안의 말을 바르게 배열하여 문장을 완성하시오.

1 그는 밤에 너무 많이 먹는다. (eat, he)
→ _____ _____ too much at night.

2 Jean과 그녀의 개는 공원에서 달리는 것을 좋아한다. (enjoy, running)
→ Jean and her dog _____ _____ at the park.

3 나의 부모님은 선생님이다. 그들은 수학을 가르친다. (be, teach)
→ My parents _____ teachers. They _____ math.

Point 03 현재 시제의 일반동사 부정문은 동사 앞에 don't/doesn't를 붙여요!

- 현재 시제의 일반동사 부정문: 「don't/doesn't + 동사원형」으로 쓴다.

주어	부정문
1, 2인칭 단·복수, 3인칭 복수 (I / You / We / They 등)	주어 + don't + 동사원형
3인칭 단수 (He / She / It 등)	주어 + doesn't + 동사원형

(축약형: do not → don't, does not → doesn't)

We don't go to school on weekends. 우리는 주말에 학교에 가지 않는다.
Susan doesn't like P.E. class. Susan은 체육 수업을 좋아하지 않는다.

Point 04 일반동사 현재형의 의문문을 만들 때는 문장 앞에 Do/Does를 붙여요!

주어	의문문	대답	
		긍정	부정
1, 2인칭 및 복수 (I/You/We/They 등)	Do + 주어 + 동사원형 ~?	Yes, 주어 + do.	No, 주어 + don't.
3인칭 단수 (He/She/It 등)	Does + 주어 + 동사원형 ~?	Yes, 주어 + does.	No, 주어 + doesn't.

Do you clean your room every day? 너는 방을 매일 청소하니?
→ Yes, I do. / No, I don't. 응, 그래 / 아니, 그렇지 않아.

Does Sam sing well? Sam은 노래를 잘 부르니?
→ Yes, he does. 응, 그래 / No, he doesn't. 응, 그래 / 아니, 그렇지 않아.

핵심만 콕! 문법 Check

A 괄호 안에서 알맞은 말을 고르시오.

1 We (aren't, don't) learn Chinese at school.

2 My younger sister doesn't (like, likes) social studies.

3 Q: (Do, Does) they have classes today?
A: No, they (don't, doesn't).

4 Q: (Do, Does) she collect stamps?
A: No, she (don't, doesn't). She collects coins.

5 Q: (Do, Does) you play tennis every Sunday?
A: Yes, (I do, you do).

B 우리말과 같은 뜻이 되도록 틀린 부분을 찾아 밑줄 긋고 어법에 맞게 고쳐 쓰시오.

1 수업은 8시에 시작하지 않는다.
→ Classes doesn't begin at 8 o'clock.   → _____

2 Rebecca는 공포영화를 좋아하지는 않는다.
→ Rebecca loves not horror movies.   → _____

3 Daniel과 Tom은 교복을 입니?
→ Does Daniel and Tom wear school uniforms?   → _____

4 Mike는 김치를 좋아하니?
→ Do Mike likes *kimchi*?   → _____

C 괄호 안의 동사를 활용하여 문장을 완성하시오.

1 Sam and Henry _____ _____ breakfast. (eat, not)

2 _____ you and Jade _____ at the zoo? (work)

3 She _____ _____ letters to me. (write, not)

D 우리말과 같은 뜻이 되도록 괄호 안의 말을 이용하여 문장을 완성하시오.

1 그의 삼촌은 야채를 기르지 않는다. (grow)
→ His uncle _____ _____ vegetables.

2 너는 엄마가 집안 일을 하는 것을 도와 드리니? (help)
→ _____ _____ _____ your mom with housework?

[1~2] 빈칸에 알맞은 말을 고르시오.

01

> _____ drinks milk every morning.

① I   ② You   ③ We
④ They   ⑤ She

02

> _____ your brother play badminton?

① Is   ② Are   ③ Am
④ Does   ⑤ Do

03 빈칸에 알맞지 <u>않은</u> 것은?

> Dora _____ music.

① likes   ② studies   ③ practices
④ doesn't play   ⑤ listen to

04 빈칸에 <u>공통으로</u> 알맞은 말은?

> • I _____ breakfast at 8 o'clock.
> • You _____ beautiful eyes.
> • Hillary doesn't _____ a cat.

① eat   ② look   ③ have
④ raise   ⑤ see

05 `서술형`

빈칸 ⓐ에 알맞은 말을 쓰시오. (단, 축약형으로 쓸 것)

> A: Does Ben like music?
> B: ⓐ _____, _____ _____.
>   But he likes P.E. class.
> A: Oh, I see.

06 다음을 부정문으로 바르게 옮긴 것은?

> Nari sings in a church choir.

① Nari don't sing in a church choir.
② Nari sings not in a church choir.
③ Nari don't sings in a church choir.
④ Nari doesn't sing in a church choir.
⑤ Nari doesn't sings in a church choir.

07 짝지어진 대화가 <u>어색한</u> 것은?

① A: Do you play chess?
   B: Yes, I do. I love it.
② A: Are you good at English?
   B: No, I'm not.
③ A: Does Jake study in the library?
   B: No, I don't.
④ A: Does she plant flowers?
   B: Yes, she does.
⑤ A: Do your sister and brother like sports?
   B: No, they don't.

08 대화의 흐름이 자연스럽도록 빈칸에 알맞은 말은?

> Man: Excuse me. Do you know Mr. Brown?
> Girl: _____.
>   He lives next to my house.

① Yes, I do.   ② Yes, I have.
③ Yes, I does.   ④ No, I don't.
⑤ No, I haven't.

09 우리말과 일치하도록 영어로 바르게 옮긴 것은?

① 그는 아침에 달린다.
  → He run in the morning.
② 호랑이는 아프리카에 살지 않는다.
  → Tigers aren't live in Africa.
③ 아빠와 나는 함께 하이킹을 한다.
  → My father and I goes hiking together.
④ 너희 선생님은 학생들에게 친절하시니?
  → Does your teacher nice to students?
⑤ Ted는 저녁 먹기 전에 숙제를 하니?
  → Does Ted do his homework before dinner?

10 서술형

다음 문장의 주어를 괄호 안의 말로 바꾸어 문장을 다시 쓰시오.

I do my homework before dinner. (She)

→ She _____

11 서술형

다음을 부정문과 의문문으로 고쳐 쓰시오.

The student studies English every day.

→ _____ (부정문)

→ _____ (의문문)

12 서술형

대화의 흐름이 자연스럽도록 빈칸에 알맞은 말을 쓰시오.

Q: What time does Bora go to bed?

→ A: She _____
  _____ at ten.

[13~14] 어법상 옳은 문장을 고르시오.

13
① Do you happy?
② She doesn't often calls me.
③ I always listen to my friends.
④ Do Alice sings along to the guitar?
⑤ He don't practices basketball in the morning.

14
① He fix my computer.
② Do you have a test today?
③ We doesn't know his name.
④ Does your parents give you pocket money?
⑤ Sally and Jacky don't goes shopping on weekdays.

[15~16] 다음을 읽고 물음에 답하시오.

Our School Art Club visits a children's hospital once a month. We (A) _____ time with the children there. Peter (B) _____ them to paint. (가) Janet folds paper with them. We are all happy there.

* fold paper: 종이 접기를 하다

15 빈 칸 (A)와 (B)에 알맞은 말이 순서대로 나열된 것은?

① spend, help
② spend, helps
③ spends, play
④ wastes, plays
⑤ waste, work

16 서술형

위 글의 (가)를 의문문으로 바꿔 쓰시오.

→ _____

17 밑줄 친 부분이 어법상 옳은 것을 <u>모두</u> 고르면?

ⓐ The bird <u>flys</u> away.
ⓑ Tim <u>plays</u> baseball in the park.
ⓒ Dana <u>watches</u> TV in the living room.
ⓓ Mom <u>washs</u> dishes after dinner.
ⓔ Chris <u>cleanes</u> his room every day.
ⓕ She <u>goes</u> to bed late.

① ⓐ, ⓒ, ⓕ　　② ⓑ, ⓒ, ⓔ　　③ ⓑ, ⓒ, ⓕ
④ ⓐ, ⓑ, ⓒ, ⓔ　　⑤ ⓑ, ⓔ, ⓕ

고난도

18 ⓐ~ⓕ에서 어법상 옳은 문장의 개수는?

ⓐ Does she read books on weekends?
ⓑ I exercises every day.
ⓒ My father gets up early in the morning.
ⓓ Are you go to middle school?
ⓔ Susan doesn't has time to have lunch.
ⓕ They make a poster for the contest.

① 2개　　② 3개　　③ 4개
④ 5개　　⑤ 6개

19 다음 표의 내용과 일치하지 <u>않는</u> 것은?

이름	Tanya	John
나이	14	15
사는 곳	California	Vancouver
등교 방법	by bus	on foot
가장 좋아하는 과목	science	math
주말에 하는 일	practice swimming	go skateboarding

① John lives in Vancouver.
② John likes math a lot.
③ Science is Tanya's favorite subject.
④ John and Tanya are the same age.
⑤ Tanya goes swimming every weekend.

신유형

20 다음 문장 ⓐ~ⓔ에서 어법상 <u>어색한</u> 곳을 찾아 바르게 고친 학생은?

ⓐ My Mom and Dad doesn't like scary movies.
ⓑ Does they come home on foot?
ⓒ A man stand at the gate.
ⓓ The woman sit on the bench.
ⓔ I stays up late at night.

① Jack: ⓐ에서 'doesn't like'를 'don't likes'로 고쳐야 해.
② Mike: ⓑ에서 'come'을 'comes'로 고쳐야 해.
③ Stan: ⓒ에서 'stand'를 'stands'로 고쳐야 해.
④ Harry: ⓓ에서 'sit'을 'sitts'로 고쳐야 해.
⑤ Rose: ⓔ에서 'stays'를 'staies'로 고쳐야 해.

[21~22] 다음 글을 읽고 물음에 답하시오.

　　Today (A) (is, are) my school's sports competition. The students usually (B) (wear, wears) school uniforms, but we (C) (don't, doesn't) wear them today. We don't have classes. Instead, we compete in some sports activities. I am a runner. My teacher (D) (tell, tells) me to stand on the starting line. I am ready to win the race!

* ready to win the race: 경주에 이길 준비가 되어 있는

21 (A)~(D)에 알맞은 말이 순서대로 나열된 것은?

① is, wears, doesn't, tells
② are, wears, doesn't, tell
③ is, wear, doesn't, tell
④ are, wears, don't, tell
⑤ is, wear, don't, tells

22 위 글을 읽고 답할 수 <u>없는</u> 질문은?

① Is the writer a student?

② Do all students wear uniforms today?

③ Do the students have classes today?

④ Do the students play sports today?

⑤ Does the writer win the race?

23 글의 밑줄 친 ①~⑤ 중 다음 표의 내용과 <u>다르게</u> 서술된 것은?

		Hyemin	Junho
On Sat.	watch TV at home	O	O
	help mom with dinner	O	X
	play soccer	X	O
On Sun.	play computer games	X	O
	go out with friends	O	O
	read books	O	X

(O: 하는 일; X: 하지 않는 일)

　　Hi, my name is Hyemin. On Saturdays, ① <u>I usually watch TV at home, and my little brother Junho does, too.</u> ② <u>We also help my mom with preparing dinner.</u> When his friends come over, ③ <u>Junho often plays soccer</u> with them. On Sundays, ④ <u>I usually go out with friends.</u> Junho usually plays computer games, but I don't. ⑤ <u>I also read books, but my brother doesn't.</u>

24 서술형

표와 내용이 일치하도록 물음에 답하시오.

	Math	Science
Tom	👍😀	👍😀
Jim	😖	👍😀
Kelly	😖	👍😀

(1) Does Tom like science?

→ _____, _____.

(2) Do Jim and Kelly like math?

→ _____, _____.

고난도

25 서술형 심화

다음은 Emma가 자신을 소개하는 글이다. 어법상 <u>어색한</u> 부분을 찾아 밑줄 긋고 바르게 고쳐 쓰시오. (3개)

　　Hi, my name is Emma. I am from England. I goes to a middle school in London. I like my school. My favorite subject is French. I speak not French well, but I practice it every day. My pen-pal write to me every week. We like each other a lot.

① _____ → _____
② _____ → _____
③ _____ → _____

CHAPTER
02

명사와 관사

명사와 관사

명사는 사람, 사물, 장소 등의 이름을 나타내는 말이다. 일정한 형태가 있어서 수를 셀 수 있느냐 없느냐에 따라, 셀 수 있는 명사와 셀 수 없는 명사로 나눌 수 있다.

관사는 명사 앞에서 명사의 수, 의미, 성격을 정하는 말이다. 관사에는 특정하게 정해지지 않은 것을 지칭하는 부정관사 a, an, 특정한 것을 지칭하는 정관사 the가 있다.

한눈에 쏙! 문법 Chart

셀 수 있는 명사	복수형	대부분	+ -s
		-s, -ch, -sh, -x, -o	+ -es
		자음 + y	y → i + -es
		모음 + y	y + -es
		-f, -fe	f, fe → v + -es
셀 수 없는 명사	추상 : 형태가 없는 감정, 개념, 가치 eg. friendship, love		
	고유 : 사람 이름, 지명, 요일 등 eg. David, Seoul, Central Park, Saturday		
	물질 : 일정한 형태가 없음 eg. water, bread		
부정 관사 a/an	셀 수 있는 명사이고, 불특정한 하나를 가리킬 때		
정관사 the	특정한 것을 가리키고, 명사의 종류나 단 · 복수와 관계 없음		

핵심만 쏙! 문법 Point

Point 01 셀 수 있는 명사의 복수형에는 보통 -s를 붙여요!

대부분의 명사	+ -s	book → books cup → cups dog → dogs
-s, -x, -ch, -sh로 끝나는 명사	+ -es	bus → buses box → boxes church → churches dish → dishes
자음 + o로 끝나는 명사	+ -es	potato → potatoes hero → heroes * 예외 piano → pianos radio → radios photo → photos
자음 + y로 끝나는 명사	y를 i로 바꾸고 + -es	baby → babies candy → candies city → cities lady → ladies
모음 + y로 끝나는 명사	+ -s	boy → boys day → days monkey → monkeys toy → toys
-f, -fe로 끝나는 명사	-f, fe를 v로 바꾸고 + -es	leaf → leaves life → lives knife → knives wife → wives * 예외 roof → roofs proof → proofs

- 셀 수 있는 명사의 복수형에는 형태가 불규칙적으로 변화하는 경우가 있다.
  man – men, woman – women, foot – feet, tooth – teeth
  child – children, mouse – mice, ox – oxen, goose – geese
- 명사 중에는 단수와 복수의 형태가 같은 명사들도 있다.
  fish – fish, sheep – sheep, deer – deer

Point 02 셀 수 없는 명사는 항상 단수형을 사용해요!

추상명사	형태가 없는 개념, 감정, 가치 등을 나타내는 명사 friendship, happiness, kindness, love, luck, peace, success, truth 등
고유명사	사람 이름, 지명, 요일과 같이 고유한 이름을 나타내는 명사 David, Seoul, Korea, Saturday, April, the Eiffel Tower, Christmas 등
물질명사	물, 공기, 설탕 등과 같이 일정한 형태가 없는 명사 air, bread, butter, coffee, milk, paper, salt, sugar, water, wood 등

Point 03 셀 수 없는 명사의 수량 표현은 측정 단위를 사용해요!

a cup of	coffee, tea	a glass of	water, milk, juice
a loaf of	bread	a slice of	bread, pizza, cheese
a bowl of	rice	a bottle of	soda, milk, juice
a piece of	cheese, paper, pizza, cake, advice, furniture, information	a box of	cereal, chocolate

Point 04 '~가 있다'는 There is + 단수명사 or There are + 복수명사를 사용해요!

- 「There is/are ...」는 '~가 있다'는 뜻으로 There is 다음에는 단수 명사, There are 다음에는 복수 명사가 온다.
  There is a bag under the desk. 책상 아래 가방이 하나 있다.
  There are many students in the classroom. 교실에 많은 학생들이 있다.

- 부정문은 「There is/are not ...」의 형태이며, '~가 있지 않다'라는 뜻이다. 축약형은 「There isn't/aren't ...」이다. 의문문은 「Is/Are there~?」의 형태이며, 대답은 「Yes, there is/are.」 또는 「No, there isn't/aren't.」로 한다.

핵심만 콕! 문법 Check

A 〈보기〉에서 빈칸에 알맞은 말을 골라 적절한 형태로 쓰시오. (한 번씩만 쓰시오.)

> **보기**
>
> knife   bike   player   leaf

1 Sally has a red _____.
2 The _____ change their colors in fall.
3 There are seven _____ and forks on the table.
4 There are nine _____ in a baseball team.

B 밑줄 친 부분이 어법상 올바르면 O표, 틀리면 바르게 고쳐 쓰시오.

1 <u>Mouses</u> love to eat cheese.   → _____
2 I see three <u>gooses</u> on the lake.   → _____
3 My sister likes <u>fishes</u>.   → _____
4 Mr. Kim has two <u>children</u>.   → _____

C 어법에 맞지 않은 부분을 찾아 전체 문장을 고쳐 쓰시오.

1 I drink two glass of orange juice every day. → _____
2 We need two bottle of waters.   → _____
3 I want three piece of cakes.   → _____
4 She needs two loafs of bread.   → _____

D 우리말과 뜻이 같도록 괄호 안의 말을 활용하여 문장을 완성하시오.

1 그 가게 안에는 많은 손님들이 있다. (customer)
→ There _____ many _____ in the store.

2 당신의 주머니 안에 동전이 조금 있나요? (coin)
→ _____ there any _____ in your pocket?

3 10월에는 휴일이 많이 있다. (holiday)
→ There _____ many _____ in October.

4 바구니 안에는 사과가 얼마나 많이 들어 있나요? (apple)
→ How many _____ _____ there in the basket?

핵심만 쏙! 문법 Point

Point 05 · 사람이나 동물의 소유격 표시는 -'s를 사용해요!

단수명사	+ 's	the cat's eyes
-s로 끝나는 복수명사	+ '	girls' high school
-s로 끝나지 않는 복수명사	+ 's	the children's bags

■ 무생물의 소유격은 the + 소유되는 명사 + of + 소유하는 명사로 쓴다.
the door of the house (그 집의 문)　　　the cover of the book (그 책의 표지)

Point 06 · 셀 수 있는 명사이고 불특정한 하나를 가리킬 때, 단수명사 앞에 부정관사 a 또는 an을 사용해요!

I have a brother and two sisters. 나는 남동생 하나, 여동생 둘이 있다. → 하나(=one)의
She is a teacher. 그녀는 선생님이다. → 여럿 중 막연한 하나
I play soccer once a week. 나는 매주 마다 한 번 축구를 한다. → ~마다(=per)
A dog is a friendly animal. 개는 친근한 동물이다. → 종족 대표

Point 07 · 정관사 the는 '특정한 것'을 가리키고, 명사의 종류나 단/복수 상관없이 쓰여요!

앞에 나온 명사를 다시 말할 때	She has a cell phone. The cell phone is very nice.
서로 알고 있는 특정 명사를 가리킬 때	Please close the window.
명사 뒤에 수식어구가 있을 때	The book on the chair is mine.
세상에서 유일한 것을 말할 때	the Sun, the moon, the Earth, the universe, the world, the north, the east
악기 이름 앞에	She plays the piano very well.
서수, 최상급 앞에	Terry is the smartest boy in the class.
only, same, last 앞에	the only man, the same number, the last time
종족 전체를 대표할 때	The cat can run fast.
자연환경 앞에	the sea, the sky, the ground, the weather

Point 08 · 아래의 경우에는 관사를 쓰지 않아요!

고유명사 앞	My friend's name is Gloria. She lives in France.
운동경기 앞	We play soccer/tennis/basketball.
과목명 앞	Math is difficult.
식사 이름 앞	I didn't have breakfast/lunch/dinner.
계절 이름 앞	Spring comes after winter.
질병 이름 앞	My grandmother died of cancer.
by + 교통수단	I go there by bus/subway/train.

■ 시설물이 본래의 목적으로 사용될 때에는, 시설물 앞에 관사를 쓰지 않는다.

go to school (공부하러) 학교에 가다　　go to bed (자러) 잠자리에 들다　　go to church (예배 드리러) 교회에 가다

핵심만 콕! 문법 Check

A 괄호 안에서 알맞은 말을 고르시오.

1 Can you close (a, the) door over there, please?
2 Did you write (a, the) memo on the desk?
3 (An, The) Earth goes around the Sun.
4 Brian plays (a, the) cello very well.

B 밑줄 친 부분이 어법상 올바르면 O표, 틀리면 바르게 고쳐 쓰시오.

1 They play badminton together. → _____
2 The autumn is my favorite season. → _____
3 I have breakfast at 7 in the morning. → _____
4 Most people go to Jeju Island by the plane. → _____

C 우리말과 뜻이 같도록 빈칸에 a, an 또는 the를 쓰시오.

1 여기는 너무 더워요. 창문을 열어주세요.
→ It's too hot here. Open _____ window behind you, please.

2 그는 딸이 한 명 있는데 그 딸은 유명한 작가이다.
→ He has _____ daughter, and _____ daughter is a famous writer.

3 아빠는 거실에 엄마는 부엌에 계신다.
→ Dad is in _____ living room and Mom is in _____ kitchen.

D 우리말과 뜻이 같도록 괄호 안의 말을 바르게 배열하여 문장을 완성하시오.

1 이 나무의 이름은 무엇인가요? (this tree, the name, of)
→ What is _____ ?

2 나에게 그 이야기의 결말을 이야기해 주세요. (of, the story, the ending)
→ Please tell me _____ .

01 명사의 단수형과 복수형이 잘못 짝지어진 것은?

① box - boxes ② ox - oxen

③ man - men ④ roof - rooves

⑤ month – months

02 서술형

괄호 안의 말을 활용하여 우리말을 영어로 옮겨 쓰시오.

Chris는 밥 두 공기를 먹는다. (eat, bowl, rice)

→ _____

03 빈칸에 부정관사 a를 쓸 수 없는 것을 모두 고르면?

① I am _____ Mr. Park.

② He has _____ orange.

③ His father is _____ doctor.

④ There is _____ coin on the table.

⑤ There is _____ magazine on the sofa.

04 밑줄 친 부분 중 어법상 옳지 않은 것은?

A: ① Are ② there some orange juice ③ in the fridge?

B: Yes, ④ there is. We have ⑤ three pieces of pizza, too.

최다빈출

05 짝지어진 대화가 어색한 것은?

① A: Are there many trees in the garden?
   B: Yes, there are.

② A: Is there a pen on the table?
   B: No, it isn't. There is nothing on the table.

③ A: Is there a bag on the bed?
   B: No, there isn't a bag on the bed.

④ A: Are there two pairs of shoes under the table?
   B: No, there aren't.

⑤ A: Are there books about science?
   B: Yes, there are some books about science.

최다빈출

06 어법상 옳은 것은?

① There are leaves on the street.

② Three sheeps are on the farm.

③ She has four puppys in her house.

④ The old man has three sweet potatos.

⑤ There are seven man at the bus stop.

07 서술형

우리말과 뜻이 같도록 어법상 틀린 부분을 찾고 바르게 고쳐 쓰시오.

ⓐ I live in the Seoul. (나는 서울에 산다.)

ⓑ He wants a glasses of water.
   (그는 물 한 잔을 원한다.)

ⓐ: _____ → _____

ⓑ: _____ → _____

08 빈칸에 정관사 the가 들어갈 수 <u>없는</u> 것은?
(대소문자 상관 없음)

① He wants _____ red cap.
② Who is _____ girl at the door?
③ _____ Sun is bigger than the Earth.
④ Do you like _____ program?
⑤ I eat _____ breakfast at 7.

09 밑줄 친 부정관사 a와 그 쓰임이 같은 것은?

Sarah goes swimming twice <u>a</u> week.

① She is <u>a</u> nurse.
② A dolphin is <u>a</u> clever animal.
③ There is <u>a</u> sofa in my room.
④ <u>A</u> man gave me some coins.
⑤ I play the guitar an hour <u>a</u> day.

10 서술형

〈보기〉의 단어를 활용하여 빈칸에 알맞은 말을 쓰시오.

┌─ 보기 ─────────────────────┐
│ cup   water   bottle   tea │
└───────────────────────────┘

(1) 저에게 물 두 병을 건네 주세요.
→ Please pass me _____
_____.

(2) 나의 어머니는 아침마다 차 한잔을 마신다.
→ My mother drinks _____
_____ every morning.

11 대화의 빈칸에 들어갈 수 <u>없는</u> 것은?

A: What do you see under the table?
B: I see a pair of _____.

① gloves   ② shoes   ③ glass
④ pants   ⑤ jeans

12 빈칸에 알맞지 <u>않은</u> 것은?

There are _____ in the kitchen.

① many oranges
② seven puppies
③ a slice of cheese
④ three bananas
⑤ two bottles of water

13 밑줄 친 there의 뜻이 나머지와 <u>다른</u> 하나는?

① <u>There</u> is a pen on the desk.
② Look at the cat over <u>there</u>.
③ <u>There</u> isn't any money here.
④ Is <u>there</u> some milk in the fridge?
⑤ <u>There</u> are too many people outside.

고난도

14 어법에 맞는 문장을 <u>모두</u> 고르면?

ⓐ I want a cup of coffees.
ⓑ I need a piece of shoes.
ⓒ She drinks two bottle of water every day.
ⓓ We all have a slice of pizza.
ⓔ Please give me a piece of advice.
ⓕ I need a pair of black socks.

① ⓐ, ⓒ   ② ⓑ, ⓓ   ③ ⓒ, ⓓ, ⓔ
④ ⓒ, ⓔ, ⓕ   ⑤ ⓓ, ⓔ, ⓕ

15 대화의 흐름이 자연스럽도록 빈칸에 알맞은 말이 순서대로 나열된 것은?

A: It's so hot here. Turn on _____ air conditioner, please.
B: It's broken. Let's open _____ window.

① the - an
② an - a
③ the - the
④ 필요 없음 - the
⑤ a - the

16 짝지어진 관계가 나머지 넷과 <u>다른</u> 하나는?

① fox - foxes
② do - does
③ city - cities
④ wolf - wolves
⑤ lady - ladies

17 서술형

〈보기〉의 단어를 활용하여 빈칸에 알맞은 말을 쓰시오.

┌─ 보기 ─────────────────────┐
│ piece   loaf   slice │
│ cup   bottle   pair │
└────────────────────────────┘

(1) The child needs two _____ of socks.
(2) Will you give me a _____ of advice?
(3) I want two _____ of pizza and a glass of soda.
(4) Four _____ of bread and two _____ of coffee, please.

18 서술형

주어진 어구를 재배열하여 문장을 만들 때, <u>세 번째로</u> 오는 것은?

Jenny는 하루에 우유를 두 잔씩 마신다.
(Jenny, two glasses of, drinks, a day, milk)

→ _____

19 빈칸에 the를 쓸 수 <u>없는</u> 것의 개수는?

ⓐ _____ two men are my cousins.
ⓑ We go there by _____ bus.
ⓒ Please open _____ window.
ⓓ Do you know _____ pretty girl?
ⓔ The family lives in _____ Seoul.
ⓕ She has a garden in her house. _____ garden is really beautiful.

① 2개
② 3개
③ 4개
④ 5개
⑤ 6개

20 a, an, the 중에서 빈칸에 알맞은 말을 쓰시오.
(단, 필요 없으면 X표 하시오.)

Let me tell you about my school life. I usually get up early in ⓐ _____ morning. I go to ⓑ _____ school at 8. I play the piano in my music class. In my P.E. class, I play ⓒ _____ soccer with my friends. I love my school life. It is a lot of fun. How is yours?

21 빈칸에 알맞은 말이 〈보기〉와 <u>다른</u> 하나는?

┌─ 보기 ─────────────────────┐
│ The Earth goes around _____ Sun. │
└────────────────────────────┘

① _____ cake on the table is for you.
② I have a puppy. _____ puppy is so cute.
③ Amy plays _____ piano every Saturday.
④ I'm so cold. Close _____ door, please.
⑤ Her favorite subject is _____ English.

22 빈칸에 알맞은 말이 순서대로 나열된 것은?

> • There (A) _____ a table in the room.
> • There (B) _____ two chairs next to the table.
> • There (C) _____ some oranges on the table.
> • There (D) _____ no water on the table.

① is, are, is, are
② is, is, is, are
③ is, are, are, are
④ is, are, are, is
⑤ is, are, is, is

 고난도

23 ⓐ~ⓔ는 어법상 <u>잘못된</u> 문장이다. ⓐ~ⓔ를 바르게 고친 학생은?

> ⓐ I want two loaf of bread.
> ⓑ Potatos are good for you.
> ⓒ There is many people on the bus.
> ⓓ There are an art museum in this city.
> ⓔ Did you see two mouses in the hole?

① Julie: ⓐ에서 loaf를 loaves로 고쳐야 해.
② Harry: ⓑ에서 Potatos를 Potato로 고쳐야 해.
③ Jerry: ⓒ에서 people을 peoples로 고쳐야 해.
④ Lucy: ⓓ에서 an을 빼야 해.
⑤ Tom: ⓔ에서 mouses를 mouse로 고쳐야 해.

24 서술형

밑줄 친 우리말을 영어로 옮길 때 빈칸에 알맞은 말을 쓰시오.

> M: This is Grace Hotel. May I help you?
> W: Yes. I need a room for two people from October 1 to October 3.
> M: OK. We have a special room with an ocean view. It has two beds and a bathroom. <u>발코니에는 작은 정원도 하나 있습니다.</u>
> W: Sounds good. Can I book it?
>
> * a room with an ocean view: 바다가 보이는 전망이 좋은 방
> * book: (식당, 호텔 등에) 예약하다

→ _____ _____
also _____ _____
_____ on the balcony.

 고난도

25 서술형 심화

Based on the picture, rewrite the sentence correctly.

① There are two glasses of water.
→ _____

② There is a piece of cheese.
→ _____

③ There is a loaf of bread.
→ _____

④ There are many oranges.
→ _____

⑤ There is a cup of coffee.
→ _____

CHAPTER

03

대명사

대명사

사람이나 사물의 이름을 나타내는 말이 명사이다. 대명사는 바로 이러한 명사를 대신하여 쓸 수 있는 말이다. 대명사에는 '이 사람/이것(this)', '저 사람/저것(that)'과 같이 특정한 사람이나 사물을 가리키는 지시대명사, 특정하지 않은 사람이나 사물을 가리키는 부정대명사, -self 또는 -selves를 붙여 '~자신(들)'이라고 해석하는 재귀대명사 등이 있다.

- **대명사의 종류**

인칭대명사	I, we, you, he, she, it, they
지시대명사	this, that, these, those
부정대명사	one, some, any, all, every 등
재귀대명사	myself, yourself, himself, herself, itself, ourselves, yourselves, themselves

한눈에 쏙! 문법 Chart

		인칭	인칭대명사	재귀대명사
인칭대명사 재귀대명사	단수	1인칭	I	myself
		2인칭	you	yourself
		3인칭	he	himself
			she	herself
			it	itself
	복수	1인칭	we	ourselves
		2인칭	you	yourselves
		3인칭	they	themselves
지시대명사	단수	가까운 곳		this
		먼 곳		that
	복수	가까운 곳		these
		먼 곳		those
부정대명사	one		이전에 언급된 하나의 불특정 대상	
	some		+ 단수/복수 명사(긍정문, 의문문)	
	any		+ 단수/복수 명사(부정문, 의문문, 조건문, 긍정문)	

핵심만 쏙! 문법 Point

Point 01 지시대명사는 가까이 혹은 멀리 있는 특정 사람/사물을 가리킬 때 사용해요!

- 지시대명사는 가까이 혹은 멀리 있는 특정한 사람이나 사물을 가리킬 때 사용하며, 단수(하나)일 때와 복수(둘 이상)일 때 그 형태가 다르다.

	단수	복수
거리상 가까이 있을 때	this (이 사람/이것)	these (이 사람들/이것들)
거리상 멀리 있을 때	that (저 사람/저것)	those (저 사람들/저것들)

This is Tom. 이 사람은 Tom이다.

That is a rainbow. 저것은 무지개다.

These are English storybooks. 이것들은 영어동화책들이다.

Those are my classmates. 저 사람들은 내 학급친구들이다.

- **지시형용사 this, that:** '이~', '저~'라는 뜻으로 명사 앞에서 명사를 꾸며주는 지시형용사로도 쓰인다.

Point 02 비인칭 주어 it은 '그것'으로 해석하지 않아요!

- 비인칭 주어 it은 시간, 거리, 날짜, 요일, 날씨, 계절, 온도, 명암 등을 나타낼 때 쓴다.

- 비인칭 주어 it은 따로 '그것'이라고 해석하지 않는다.

시간	It's 3 o'clock. 세 시이다.	날씨	It's sunny. 날씨가 맑다.
거리	It's 100 meters away. 100미터 떨어져 있다.	계절	It's spring. 봄이다.
날짜	It's December 2nd. 12월 2일이다.	온도	It's cold in winter. 겨울에는 춥다.
요일	It's Friday. 금요일이다.	명암	It's dark now. 지금은 어둡다.

Point 03 지시대명사 it과 비인칭 주어 it은 서로 달라요!

- **지시대명사 it:** 특정한 단수 명사를 지칭하거나 이전에 언급된 동일한 단수 명사를 가리킬 때 사용하며, '그것'이라고 해석한다.

It is red. 그것은 빨간색이다. (지시대명사 it)

I lost my pen. I can't find it. 나는 펜을 잃어버렸다. 나는 그것을 찾을 수 없다. (지시대명사 it = my pen)

- 지시대명사 it은 대명사 this와 that을 대신해서도 쓸 수 있다.

- **비인칭 주어 it:** 주어가 불명확하거나 주어가 없는 불완전한 문장에서 주어 역할을 한다. '그것'이라고 따로 해석하지 않으며, 거리, 날짜, 요일, 날씨, 계절, 온도, 명암 등을 나타낼 때 쓴다.

It is cloudy. 날씨가 흐리다. (비인칭 주어 it: 날씨)

It is Sunday. 일요일이다. (비인칭 주어 it: 요일)

핵심만 콕! 문법 Check

A 괄호 안에서 알맞은 말을 고르시오.

1 Whose jacket is (this, that) over there?
2 I like (this, these) white jeans.
3 (This, These) is not his idea. It is (me, my, mine).
4 What are (this, these)? — They are toys for my younger brother.

B 우리말과 뜻이 같도록 밑줄 친 부분을 어법에 맞게 고쳐 쓰시오.

1 <u>These</u> is hot. (이것은 뜨겁다.) → _____
2 <u>Those</u> is Jane's. (저것은 Jane의 것이다.) → _____
3 Are <u>that</u> his pet dogs? (저것들은 그의 애완견들이니?) → _____

C 괄호 안의 말을 바르게 배열하여 문장을 완성하고, it이 지시대명사인지 비인칭 주어인지 구별하여 O표 하시오.

1 밖에 바람이 분다. (is, windy, outside, it)
→ _____ (지시대명사, 비인칭 주어)

2 여름에는 매우 덥다. (hot, it, very, is)
→ _____ in summer. (지시대명사, 비인칭 주어)

3 그것은 나의 중학교이다. (middle school, is, my, it)
→ _____ (지시대명사, 비인칭 주어)

4 저기에 흰색 차가 있다. 그것은 내 것이다. (mine, is, it)
→ There's a white car over there. _____ (지시대명사, 비인칭 주어)

D 우리말과 뜻이 같도록 빈칸에 알맞은 말을 쓰시오.

1 저 책들이 한국에서 베스트셀러들이다.
→ _____ _____ are best-sellers in Korea.

2 그의 생일은 언제이니? 8월 28일이야.
→ When is his birthday? _____ _____ on August 28th.

3 우산을 가져가라. 밖에 비가 오고 있다.
→ Take an umbrella with you. _____ _____ _____ outside.

4 에어컨을 켜자. 너무 덥다.
→ Let's turn on the air conditioner. _____ _____ very _____.

핵심만 쏙! 문법 Point

Point 04 one은 불특정한 사물이나 일반인을 가리켜요!

- **부정대명사**: 특정하지 않은 사람이나 사물을 가리키는 대명사이다.

- 부정대명사 one은 이전에 언급된 명사와 종류는 같으나 정해지지 않은 막연한 대상을 가리킬 때 사용하며, 복수형은 ones이다.
  I need a pencil. Do you have one? 나는 연필이 필요해. 너 하나 가지고 있니? (one = a pencil)
  He doesn't like black pants. He likes blue ones.
  그는 검정색 바지를 좋아하지 않는다. 그는 파란색(바지)을 좋아한다. (ones = pants)

Point 05 some은 대부분의 긍정문/권유문에, any는 부정문/의문문에 사용해요!

- 부정대명사 some, any는 '얼마간(의), 약간(의), 조금(의), 몇몇, 어떤'이라는 뜻이다. some과 any는 형용사로도 쓰일 수 있고, 셀 수 있는 명사와 셀 수 없는 명사 둘 다에 쓸 수 있다.
  Some of the pencils in the pencil case are short. 필통에 있는 몇몇 연필은 짧다. (부정대명사)
  Some people say that the school uniforms are comfortable.
  어떤 사람들은 교복이 편하다고 말한다. (형용사 some)
  Do any of us know the password? 우리 중의 누군가 그 비밀번호를 아니? (부정대명사)

- 부정대명사 some은 주로 긍정문에, any는 부정문이나 의문문, 조건문에 주로 쓰인다.

- **기타 쓰임**: some이 의문문에, any가 긍정문에 사용되는 경우는 다음과 같다.
  Would you like some orange juice? 오렌지 주스 좀 드시겠습니까? (권유)
  Any student can do it. 어떤 학생이라도 그것을 할 수 있다. (any: 어떤 ~라도)

Point 06 재귀대명사가 생략이 가능하면 강조용법, 불가능하면 재귀용법이에요!

- **재귀대명사의 재귀용법**: 한 문장 안에서 주어와 목적어가 동일한 대상일 때 동사나 전치사의 목적어로 재귀대명사를 쓰며 '~자신(들)/ 스스로'라고 해석한다.
  The new student introduced himself. 그 신입생은 자기 자신을 소개했다.
  Love yourself. 너 자신을 사랑하라. (명령문의 주어는 'you'이다.)

- **재귀대명사의 강조용법**: 재귀대명사가 문장의 주어나 목적어와 동격으로 사용되어 그 의미를 강조하기도 한다. 이 때의 재귀대명사는 강조하는 말 바로 뒤나 문장 맨 끝에 오며, 생략해도 (강조의 의미는 사라지나) 문장은 성립한다.
  I fixed the computer myself. = I myself fixed the computer. 내가 직접 그 컴퓨터를 수리했다.
  (강조용법: myself가 주어 I를 강조)

- 재귀대명사의 형태: 인칭대명사의 소유격이나 목적격에 –self나 –selves를 붙여서 만든다.

인칭	단수	복수
1인칭	myself	ourselves
2인칭	yourself	yourselves
3인칭	himself / herself / itself	themselves

핵심만 콕! 문법 Check

A 괄호 안에서 알맞은 말을 고르시오.

1 I don't have an eraser. Can I borrow (one, ones)?

2 I need new shoes. My old (one, ones) are too small.

3 I love ice cream. (Any, Some) flavor is OK for me.

4 There are (any, some) french fries on the table.

5 My grandmother sometimes talks to (himself, herself).

B 밑줄 친 부분이 가리키는 것을 앞에서 찾아 쓰시오.

1 I need a new hat. Please buy <u>one</u> for me.　　　→ _____

2 Do you have a large bag or a small <u>one</u>?　　　→ _____

3 Those boots are expensive. Do you have cheap <u>ones</u>?　→ _____

C 밑줄 친 부분에 유의하여 다음 문장을 우리말로 해석하시오.

1 I love <u>myself</u>.　　　　　　　　　　　→ _____

2 The news <u>itself</u> is very interesting.　　　→ _____

3 Please talk about <u>yourself</u>.　　　　　　→ _____

D 우리말과 뜻이 같도록 빈칸에 알맞은 말을 쓰시오.

1 책장에 많은 책들이 있다. 나는 한 권을 빌릴 것이다.

→ There are many _____ on the bookshelf. I will _____ _____.

2 내 양말은 낡았다. 엄마가 나를 위해 새것들을 사주실 것이다.

→ My _____ are old. My mom will buy _____ _____ for
_____.

3 그 KTX에는 빈 자리가 없다.

→ There aren't _____ empty seats in the KTX.

4 그 게임들 중 어떤 것들은 정말 재미있다.

→ _____ of the games are very exciting.

[1~2] 빈칸에 알맞은 말을 고르시오.

01

> Do you have a towel? I need _____.

① one ② some ③ any
④ them ⑤ ones

02

> There is a lot of juice in the fridge. I want to drink _____.

① any ② ones ③ one
④ it ⑤ some

03 대화의 빈칸에 알맞은 말은?

> A: Can I borrow your pencil?
> B: Sure, you can use _____.

① any ② some ③ it
④ ones ⑤ one

04 빈칸에 <u>공통으로</u> 알맞은 말은?

> • _____ _____ my classroom.
> • _____ _____ my best friend, Jack.

① She is ② This is ③ They are
④ These are ⑤ Those are

05 서술형

우리말과 뜻이 같도록 빈칸에 알맞은 대명사를 쓰시오.

> 그 소녀는 노란색 장미를 좋아하지 않는다. 그녀는 빨간색(장미)을 좋아한다.
> The girl doesn't like yellow roses. She likes red _____.

최다빈출

06 밑줄 친 It의 쓰임이 나머지 넷과 <u>다른</u> 하나는?

① <u>It</u> is almost 10 p.m.
② <u>It</u> is chilly in autumn.
③ <u>It</u> is an exciting movie.
④ <u>It</u> is warm and sunny today.
⑤ What time is <u>it</u> now?

07 서술형

주어진 문장을 지시대로 바꾸어 쓰시오.

> This is a delicious orange. (복수형으로)

→ _____ _____ _____ _____.

[8~9] 밑줄 친 부분의 쓰임이 나머지 넷과 <u>다른</u> 하나는?

08

① Is <u>it</u> cold?
② <u>It</u> is summer.
③ <u>It</u> is Friday today.
④ Don't worry. <u>It</u> is not your fault.
⑤ Is <u>it</u> far from here to the public library?

09

① I made this <u>myself</u>.

② Tony calls <u>himself</u> a prince.

③ Jenny grows vegetables <u>herself</u>.

④ We made the sandwiches <u>ourselves</u>.

⑤ The students will join the contest <u>themselves</u>.

10 서술형

괄호 안의 말을 재배열하여 문장을 완성하시오.

> 그 대회의 우승자들은 그들 자신을 자랑스러워 한다.
> (the winners, of, are, the contest, proud, themselves, of)

→ _____

11 밑줄 친 ①~⑤중 어법상 틀린 것을 모두 고르면? (2개)

> Teacher: Do you have ① <u>any</u> questions for the project?
> Boy: ② <u>Yes</u>, I have ③ <u>any</u>.
> Teacher: What about you, Linda?
> Girl: ④ <u>No</u>, I don't have ⑤ <u>some</u>.

12 밑줄 친 부분이 어법상 틀린 것은?

① Please do it by <u>yourself</u>.

② I'll introduce <u>myself</u> to you.

③ He will do the work <u>herself</u>.

④ The woman lives in Seoul by <u>herself</u>.

⑤ They cleaned the classroom <u>themselves</u>.

13 서술형

우리말과 뜻이 같도록 빈칸에 알맞은 말을 쓰시오.

> Amy의 엄마는 그녀의 아들을 직접 학교에 데려다 준다.
> → Amy's mother takes her son to school
> _____.

[14~15] 빈칸에 공통으로 알맞은 말을 고르시오.
(단, 대소문자 무시)

14

> A: Look out the window. _____ is snowing.
> B: Wow! I feel like _____ is really winter now.

① one   ② any   ③ that

④ it   ⑤ this

15

> • Are there _____ cookies in the jar?
> • Nick doesn't read _____ comic books.

① these   ② any   ③ that

④ those   ⑤ this

[16~17] 우리말과 뜻이 같도록 괄호 안의 말을 활용하여 문장을 완성하시오. (필요시 형태 변경 가능)

16 서술형

> Junho는 약간의 동전을 가지고 있다. (have, coins)

→ Junho _____ _____ _____.

17 서술형

이 컵은 더러워요. 깨끗한 것 있나요? (clean)

→ This cup is dirty. Do you have _____
_____ _____?

18 밑줄 친 부분이 어법상 옳지 <u>않은</u> 것은?

① My dad fixed the car <u>himself</u>.
② Look at <u>this</u> in my hand.
③ I baked cookies. Would you like <u>some</u>?
④ I lost my cell phone. I need a new <u>one</u>.
⑤ Are <u>this</u> presents for him?

19 빈칸에 'one'이 들어갈 수 <u>없는</u> 것은?

① I need a fork.
　Please give me _____.
② I don't like this.
　Show me another _____.
③ Do you have my pen?
　— Yes, I have _____.
④ Tim's watch doesn't work.
　He needs a new _____.
⑤ My brother gave me this T-shirt.
　He got a new _____.

20 서술형

다음 질문에 완전한 영어 문장으로 답하시오.

A: What day is it today?
B: _____

21 서술형

그림과 일치하도록 괄호 안의 말을 활용하여 영작하시오.
(비인칭주어 it을 꼭 사용하고, 필요하면 괄호 안의 말의 형태를 바꾸시오.)

(1)

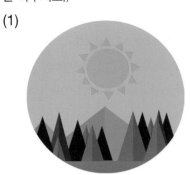

→ _____

(sun)

(2)

→ _____

(cloud, rain)

(3)

→ _____

(five, o'clock)

22 서술형

그림을 보고 〈보기〉에서 빈칸에 알맞은 말을 골라 문장을 완성 하시오.

┌ 보기 ┐
| this | that | these | those |

(1)

→ _____ _____ my shoes.

(2)

→ _____ _____ my laptop.

(3)

→ Look over there! _____
_____ my new bicycle.

23 대화의 밑줄 친 ①~⑤ 중 어법상 틀린 것은?

A: How ① was Jinsu's birthday party?
B: ② It was great. We enjoyed ③ ourself a lot.
A: Good. ④ When is your birthday party?
B: ⑤ It is on May 17th.

24 밑줄 친 부분 중 생략할 수 있는 것을 모두 고르면? (2개)

① Please help yourself.
② I make my clothes myself.
③ She can take care of herself.
④ The man hurt himself yesterday.
⑤ The children sang songs themselves.

고난도

25 서술형 심화

빈칸에 알맞은 말을 〈보기〉에서 골라 쓰시오.

┌ 보기 ┐
| myself | one | this | it |
| themselves | some | any |

(1) _____ is the new student in my class. Her name is Susie Kim. New students always introduce (2) _____ to the class. She is from Chicago. (3) _____ of the old students are from Chicago, too. They were very happy to meet each other. Susie likes to play the guitar and sing pop songs. Me, too! I actually learn how to play the guitar by (4) _____. (5) _____ is not easy, but it is exciting. In class, students need to write notes, but Susie doesn't have (6) _____ pencils. So I lend her (7)_____.

CHAPTER
04

시제

시제

어떤 일이 언제 어떤 식으로 일어나는지 시간 관계를 나타내는 것을 시제라 한다. 영어 문장에서 시제는 동사의 형태를 변화시켜 나타낸다. 이 때, 동사의 형태는 규칙적으로 변하는 경우와 불규칙적으로 변하는 경우가 있다.

• 단순 시제 *vs.* 진행형

단순 현재	I **go** to school by bus every day. 나는 매일 버스를 타고 학교에 간다.
단순 과거	I **went** to school by bus yesterday. 나는 어제 버스를 타고 학교에 갔다.
현재진행	I **am going to** school by bus now. 나는 지금 버스를 타고 학교에 가는 중이다.
과거진행	I **was going to** school by bus then. 나는 그때 버스를 타고 학교에 가는 중이었다.

한눈에 쏙! 문법 Chart

시제	적용	문장의 형태
현재	• 현재의 사실/상태, 습관적 행위, 불변의 진리, 과학적 사실, 속담, 격언 • 확정된 가까운 미래의 일	• 주어 + am/are/is • 주어 + 일반동사 원형 (3인칭 단수일 때는 '주어 + 일반동사원형-(e)s')
현재진행	• 현재 일시적으로 진행 중인 동작 (소유, 감정, 인지동사는 진행형으로 쓰지 않는다)	• 주어 + am/are/is + 일반동사원형-ing
과거	• 과거의 상태나 일어났던 일 (주로 과거를 나타내는 시간부사가 있다)	• 주어 + was/were • 주어 + 일반동사 과거형
과거진행	• 과거에 잠시 진행되었던 동작	• 주어 + was/were + 일반동사원형-ing

핵심만 쏙! 문법 Point

Point 01 현재시제는 현재의 상태나 반복적인 동작을 나타내요!

- **단순 현재:** 현재의 사실/상태, 습관적인 행위, 불변의 진리, 속담 및 격언, 과학적 사실을 나타낼 때 사용한다.
  Rick rides a bike to school. Rick은 학교에 자전거를 타고 간다. (습관적인 행위)
  Walls have ears. 벽에도 귀가 있다. (낮 말은 새가 듣고 밤 말은 쥐가 듣는다.) (속담)

- **가까운 미래를 나타내는 단순 현재:** 변경될 가능성이 거의 없이 이미 확정된 가까운 미래의 일(예: 교통 시간표, 공적인 일정 등)은 단순 현재로 나타낸다. 즉, 동사의 형태는 현재형이지만, 의미는 미래를 나타낸다.
  The train leaves at 2:15. 기차는 2시 15분에 출발한다.

Point 02 진행시제는 어느 순간에 일시적으로 진행되는 동작을 나타내요!

- **진행형:** 특정한 시점에서 진행 중인 일을 나타내고 「be동사 + 동사원형-ing」 형태로 쓴다.
- 「동사원형-ing」 형태 만드는 법

대부분의 동사	동사원형-ing	read → reading	do → doing	
-e로 끝나는 동사	e를 빼고 + -ing	come → coming make → making	bake → baking take → taking	
-ie로 끝나는 동사	-ie를 y로 바꾸고 + -ing	lie → lying	die → dying	tie → tying
「단모음 + 단자음」으로 끝나는 동사	자음을 한 번 더 쓰고 + -ing	begin → beginning stop → stopping	run → running swim → swimming	sit → sitting

- **현재진행:** '현재 일시적으로 진행 중인 동작'을 나타낸다. 「주어 + am/are/is + 동사원형-ing」로 쓰고 '~하는 중이다' 또는 '~하고 있다'로 해석한다.
  I am doing my homework now. 나는 지금 숙제를 하고 있다.
  The boys are lying on the grass. 그 소년들은 잔디 위에 누워 있다.

- **현재진행형의 부정문:** 「주어 + am/are/is + not + 동사원형-ing~.」의 형태로 쓴다. (~하고 있지 않다.)
  Betty is not doing her homework now. Betty는 지금 숙제를 하고 있지 않다.

- **현재진행형의 의문문:** 「Am/Are/Is + 주어 + 동사원형-ing~?」의 형태로 쓴다. (~하고 있니?)
  Are you talking on the phone now? — No, I'm not (talking on the phone now).
  너 지금 전화하고 있는 중이니? – 아니, 그렇지(전화를 하고있지) 않아.

Grammar Upgrade

1 단순 현재는 현재의 지속적인 상태, 반복되는 일이나 습관, 일반적인 사실 등을 나타내는 반면에, 현재진행은 지금 일시적으로 진행 중인 일을 나타낸다.
   I usually listen to music in my free time. 나는 보통 여가 시간에 음악을 듣는다. (단순현재: 습관적인 동작)
   I am listening to music now. 나는 지금 음악을 듣고 있는 중이다. (현재진행: 지금 일시적으로 진행 중인 동작)

2 진행형을 쓰지 않는 동사: 진행형은 일시적으로 진행되는 동작을 나타낸다. 따라서, have(가지고 있다), like, hate, want, know 등과 같이 소유, 감정, 상태를 나타내는 동사들은 진행형으로 쓰지 않고, 단순 시제로 쓴다.
   I like scary movies a lot. (O) 나는 무서운 영화를 매우 좋아한다.
   I am liking scary movies a lot. (X)

   cf. 단, have가 '먹다'라는 뜻이면 진행형으로 쓸 수 있다.
      I am having spaghetti. 나는 스파게티를 먹고 있는 중이다.

핵심만 콕! 문법 Check

A 괄호 안에서 알맞은 말을 고르시오.

1 Bad news (travels, is traveling) fast.

2 My big sister always (helps, is helping) my mom prepare dinner.

3 The girl (sits, is sitting) on the bench now.

4 The bird isn't (sings, singing).

5 My younger sister (isn't, doesn't) playing the piano.

6 Are the children (do, does, doing) homework? — Yes, (he is, they are).

B 어법상 어색한 곳을 찾아 바르게 고쳐 쓰시오.

1 It is taking 30 minutes from here to the subway station. _____ → _____

2 Does your father looking for his cell phone? _____ → _____

3 Do the students winning the game against the teachers? _____ → _____

4 My school is having a nice gym. _____ → _____

C 빈칸에 알맞은 말을 <보기>에서 골라 알맞은 형태로 쓰시오.

보기				
read	be	make	sleep	get

1 My dad _____ up early every morning.

2 Seoul _____ the capital of Korea.

3 The cat _____ _____ under the bed.

4 Ben and Jack _____ _____ pizza.

5 My mom _____ _____ a magazine in the living room.

D 우리말과 같은 뜻이 되도록 괄호 안의 말을 이용하여 문장을 완성하시오.

1 나의 아버지는 동물에 대해 많이 아신다. (know)

→ My father _____ a lot about animals.

2 Jimmy야, 지금 숙제하고 있니? (do)

→ Jimmy, _____ _____ _____ your homework now?

3 그 고양이가 그 개로부터 도망치고 있다. (run)

→ The cat _____ _____ away from the dog.

4 콘서트는 10분 후에 시작한다. (start)

→ The concert _____ in 10 minutes.

Point 03 be동사의 과거형은 단수일 때 was, you 혹은 복수일 때 were를 사용해요!

- be동사의 과거형은 was와 were이고 '~이었다' 또는 '(~에) 있었다'라는 뜻이다.

현재형		과거형
am, is	⟶	was
are	⟶	were

I am tired now. 나는 지금 피곤하다. → I was tired then. 나는 그때 피곤했다.
Mina is happy now. 미나는 지금 행복하다. → Mina was happy then. 미나는 그때 행복했다.
They are classmates. 그들은 학급 친구이다. → They were classmates then. 그들은 그때 학급 친구였다.

Point 04 be동사 과거형의 부정문은 not을 was/were뒤에, 의문문은 was/were를 주어 앞에 쓰여요!

- **be동사 과거형의 부정문:** 「주어 + was/were + not~.」의 형태로 쓰고 '~이 아니었다' 또는 '~에 없었다'라는 뜻이다.
The boy was not in the backyard. 소년은 뒤뜰에 없었다.
We were not middle school students last year. 우리는 작년에 중학생이 아니었다.

- **be동사 과거형의 의문문:** 「Was/Were + 주어~?」의 형태로 쓰고 '~였나요? ~에 있었나요?'라는 뜻이다. 대답은 「Yes, 주어 + was/were.」 또는 「No, 주어 + wasn't/weren't.」로 한다.
Was Sarah at home last night? Sarah는 어젯밤 집에 있었나요?
— Yes, she was. / No, she wasn't. 네, 있었어요. / 아니오, 있지 않았어요.
Were you scared at the haunted house? 너 귀신의 집에서 무서웠니?
— Yes, I was. / No, I wasn't. 네, 그랬어요. / 아니오, 그렇지 않았어요.

A 괄호 안에서 알맞은 말을 고르시오.

1 We (was, were) 13 years old then.

2 He (was, were) very busy yesterday.

3 Tom and I (am, is, are, was, were) very close friends in our childhood.

4 Jake (is, are, was, were) a player on his school basketball team last year.

B 빈칸에 알맞은 be동사의 과거형을 쓰시오.

1 The class _____ boring.

2 I _____ hungry before lunch.

3 She _____ late for school today.

4 My father and I _____ at the park.

C 질문에 알맞은 대답을 써서 대화를 완성하시오. (단, 대명사를 활용하여 답하시오.)

1 Q: Was the story interesting?

A: _____, _____ _____. I liked it a lot.

2 Q: Were you at home yesterday?

A: _____, _____ _____. I read a book at home.

3 Q: Were Mr. and Mrs. Smith interested in classical music back then?

A: _____, _____ _____. They didn't like classical music.

D 다음 문장을 〈보기〉와 같이 부정문과 의문문으로 고쳐 쓰시오.

> ┌─ 보기 ─┐
> It was very cold yesterday.
> → 부정문: It was not very cold yesterday.
> → 의문문: Was it very cold yesterday?

1 The game was exciting.

→ 부정문: _____

→ 의문문: _____

2 The questions were difficult.

→ 부정문: _____

→ 의문문: _____

Point 05 일반동사의 과거형은 '동사원형 + (e)d'로 쓰여요!

- **일반동사의 과거형**: 주어의 인칭과 수에 관계없이 「동사원형-(e)d」의 형태로 쓴다.

- **일반동사 과거형의 규칙 변화**

대부분의 일반동사	동사원형-ed	visit → visited, watch → watched
-e로 끝나는 동사	동사원형-d	invite → invited, like → liked
「자음 + y」로 끝나는 동사	y를 i로 바꾸고 + -ed	cry → cried, hurry → hurried study → studied, try → tried
「모음 + y」로 끝나는 동사	동사원형-ed	enjoy → enjoyed, play → played, stay → stayed
「단모음 + 단자음」으로 끝나는 동사	자음을 한 번 더 쓰고 + -ed	drop → dropped, stop → stopped

They moved to a new house. 그들은 새 집으로 이사했다.
Matilda studied for exams until late at night. Matilda는 밤 늦게까지 시험 공부를 했다.

- 일반동사의 과거형 중에 「동사원형-(e)d」를 쓰지 않고 형태가 바뀌는 동사들이 있다.

- **일반동사 과거형의 불규칙 변화**

	동사원형	과거형	과거분사형	뜻
A-B-B형	meet	met	met	만나다
	have	had	had	가지다
A-B-C형	do	did	done	하다
	give	gave	given	주다
A-B-A형	come	came	come	오다
	run	ran	run	달리다
A-A-A형	cut	cut	cut	자르다
	put	put	put	놓다

Point 06 일반동사 과거형의 부정문은 「주어 + didn't + 동사원형」으로, 의문문은 「Did + 주어 + 동사원형」으로 쓰여요!

- **일반동사 과거형의 부정문**: 주어의 인칭과 수에 관계없이 「주어 + didn't + 동사원형~.」으로 나타낸다.
  I didn't have breakfast this morning. 나는 오늘 아침을 안 먹었다.

- **일반동사 과거형의 의문문**: 주어의 인칭과 수에 관계없이 「Did/Didn't + 주어 + 동사원형~?」으로 나타낸다. 이 때 긍정 의문문이든 부정 의문문이든 상관없이, 대답이 긍정이면 「Yes, 주어 + did.」, 부정이면 「No, 주어 + didn't.」를 쓴다.
  Did he go to school yesterday? 그는 어제 학교에 갔었니?
  — Yes, he did. / No, he didn't. 네, 갔어요. / 아니요, 안 갔어요.
  Didn't you go to the park with your friends? 너는 친구들과 함께 공원에 가지 않니?
  — Yes, I did. / No, I didn't. 네, 갔어요. / 아니요, 안 갔어요.

핵심만 콕! 문법 Check

A   괄호 안의 말을 활용하여 과거시제의 문장으로 완성하시오

1 The child _____ for a toy. (cry)

2 Mr. Green _____ English to us last year. (teach)

3 The man _____ a rope around the tree. (tie)

4 The driver _____ the bus for passengers. (stop)

5 A guard _____ in front of the school gate. (stand)

6 My father _____ me to the shopping mall. (drive)

B   밑줄 친 동사의 과거형을 빈칸에 알맞게 쓰시오.

1 Did you <u>went</u> to the amusement park yesterday?   → _____

2 <u>Was</u> Sarah buy flowers for her mom yesterday?   → _____

3 I <u>didn't wrote</u> an email to my friend.   → _____

4 Jane and I <u>weren't go</u> to watch a movie last week.   → _____

C   우리말과 같은 뜻이 되도록 괄호 안의 말을 빈칸에 알맞은 형태로 쓰시오.

1 우리는 지난 주말에 조부모님을 방문했다. (visit)

→ We _____ our grandparents last weekend.

2 나는 내 생일 파티에 친구들을 초대했다. (invite)

→ I _____ my friends to my birthday party.

3 선생님께서 바닥에 펜을 떨어뜨리셨다. (drop)

→ The teacher _____ a pen on the floor.

D   〈보기〉와 같이 괄호 안의 말을 넣어 문장을 다시 쓰시오.

> **보기**
>
> I see the doctor. (last week) → I saw the doctor last week.

1 Dennis goes swimming. (yesterday)

→ _____

2 They have a good time. (last night)

→ _____

3 I spend time reading a book. (last weekend)

→ _____

핵심만 쏙! 문법 Point

Point 07 과거를 나타내는 시간부사가 있는 문장은 과거시제로 쓰여요!

- 과거시제의 문장에는 주로 yesterday, last ~, ago, then, at that time, in + 과거연도 등의 과거를 나타내는 시간 부사(구)들이 자주 온다.
  They went on a field trip yesterday. 그들은 어제 체험학습을 갔다.
  The bus left a few minutes ago. 버스는 몇 분 전에 떠났다.

Point 08 과거진행형은 과거 어느 시점에 진행 중이었던 동작을 나타내요!

- **과거 vs. 과거진행:** 과거시제는 과거에 이미 끝난 동작이나 역사적 사실을 나타내는 반면에, 과거진행형은 과거 어느 시점에 진행 중이었던 동작을 나타낸다.

- **과거진행형의 긍정문:** 「주어 + was/were + 동사원형-ing~.」의 형태로 쓴다.
  Jack was studying for an exam at that time. Jack은 그 때 시험을 위해 공부하는 중이었다.
  cf. Jack studied Chinese in college. Jack은 대학에서 중국어를 공부했다.

- **과거진행형의 부정문:** 「주어 + was/were + not + 동사원형-ing~.」의 형태로 쓴다.
  Jinsu was not watching TV last night. 진수는 어젯밤 TV를 보고 있지 않았다.

- **과거진행형의 의문문:** 「Was/Were + 주어 + 동사원형-ing~?」의 형태로 쓴다.
  의문사가 있는 경우는 「의문사 + was/were + 주어 + 동사원형-ing~?」의 형태로 쓴다.
  Were you taking a shower at that time? 너는 그 때 샤워를 하고 있었니?
  What were you doing in the morning? 너는 아침에 무엇을 하고 있었니?

핵심만 콕! 문법 Check

A 괄호 안에서 알맞은 말을 고르시오.

1 John studies English (on Tuesdays, last year).

2 It snowed a lot (last night, tomorrow).

3 Tina had spaghetti for lunch (yesterday, next week).

4 The train left for Busan three minutes (ago, later).

5 Mrs. Brown is growing flowers (last year, these days).

B 괄호 안에서 문맥상 가장 알맞은 것을 고르시오

1 ⓐ Jeff (reads, is reading) a book every morning.

　ⓑ Jeff (reads, was reading) a book this morning.

2 ⓐ The subway (comes, is coming)! Hurry up!

　ⓑ The subway (comes, is coming) every 10 minutes.

3 ⓐ Peter and Brenda usually (study, are studying) together.

　ⓑ Peter and Brenda (study, are studying) for their exam now.

4 ⓐ What was Tom doing? — He (played, was playing) the guitar.

　ⓑ He (played, was playing) the guitar at the Art Center in 2000.

C 밑줄 친 부분을 어법에 맞게 고쳐 쓰시오.

1 Jack <u>rides</u> his bike last Saturday.　→ _____

2 My friends and I <u>play</u> soccer after school yesterday. → _____

3 He <u>leaves</u> thirty minutes ago.　→ _____

4 She <u>sits</u> on the bench and read a book.　→ _____

D 〈보기〉와 같이 진행형으로 바꾸어 쓰시오. (단, 주어진 문장의 시제에 따르시오.)

> **보기**
>
> I ate lunch.　→　I was eating lunch.

1 Janet looked for a key.　→ _____

2 Jessica listens to music.　→ _____

3 They sang and danced.　→ _____

4 The boy climbed the tree.　→ _____

5 The bird flew in the sky.　→ _____

6 The old lady sits on a chair.　→ _____

01 동사원형과 과거형이 바르게 연결된 것은?

① hit — hitted   ② have — haved

③ stop — stoped   ④ stay — stayed

⑤ read — readed

02 [서술형]

다음 퍼즐을 완성할 때 색칠된 곳에 들어갈 단어를 쓰시오.

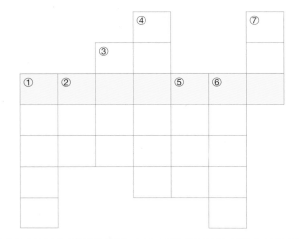

〈세로 방향으로 넣기〉

① begin의 과거형   ② run의 과거형

③ take의 과거형   ④ teach의 과거형

⑤ give의 과거형   ⑥ hear의 과거형

⑦ cut의 과거형

→ _____

03 어법상 옳은 문장은?

① I goed fishing with my father.

② Mother gived me pocket money.

③ Jane drinked milk from the bottle.

④ The teacher talked to the students.

⑤ Mike drived his car to the sports complex.

04 빈칸에 알맞은 말이 나머지와 <u>다른</u> 하나는?

① I _____ very busy yesterday.

② Peter and I _____ very fast then.

③ He _____ very happy last night.

④ _____ your friend in the library then?

⑤ My brother _____ short last year.

05 대화의 흐름이 자연스럽도록 빈칸에 알맞은 말은?

A: _____
B: No, I didn't. I went hiking.

① Did Sarah tell you the story?

② Does Susie go hiking with you?

③ Do you watch the movie, 'Iron Man'?

④ Do you and your sister study together?

⑤ Didn't you go shopping with friends last Sunday?

06 짝지어진 대화가 자연스러운 것은?

① A: Does Tina like music?
   B: Yes, she does.

② A: Is Jane playing tennis?
   B: Yes, she does.

③ A: Does Tom like a dog?
   B: No, he didn't.

④ A: Are they cleaning the classroom?
   B: Yes, they were.

⑤ A: Are you doing your homework?
   B: No, you aren't.

[7~9] 어법상 어색한 것을 고르시오.

07

① Mina is making spaghetti.
② They are rode bicycles.
③ I am drinking orange juice.
④ Mom is cutting vegetables for salad.
⑤ The old woman is sitting on the chair.

08

① Lily is swimming in the pool.
② Susan is dancing on the stage.
③ She is wanting something hot.
④ Mike never comes to school late.
⑤ My brother is playing the piano.

09

① Do whales live in groups?
② The rabbit didn't saw the tiger.
③ Jim and Sally don't go swimming.
④ My father plays tennis every Saturday.
⑤ They all left the city because of the pollution.

10 서술형

우리말과 일치하도록 빈칸에 주어진 철자로 시작하는 알맞은
단어를 쓰시오.

그 도서관은 오전 9시에 열고 오후 6시에 닫는다.
→ The library o_____ at 9 a.m. and
   c_____ at 6 p.m.

11 서술형

〈보기〉와 같이 주어진 문장을 바꿔 쓰시오.

보기
She rides a bike.
→ She doesn't ride a bike.
→ Does she ride a bike?

They are studying math now.

→ _____
→ _____

고난도

12 어법에 옳은 문장을 모두 고르면?

ⓐ Is your sister like dancing?
ⓑ Did the students have a class?
ⓒ Does Mike and Jack play soccer?
ⓓ Do your father read a newspaper?
ⓔ Are you having lunch?
ⓕ Susie isn't watching TV.

① ⓐ, ⓑ, ⓒ   ② ⓐ, ⓑ, ⓔ   ③ ⓑ, ⓓ, ⓕ
④ ⓑ, ⓔ, ⓕ   ⑤ ⓓ, ⓔ, ⓕ

13 Tom의 일정표와 일치하지 않는 것은?

Mon.	play soccer
Tue.	go swimming
Wed.	take a math test
Thur.	★ Today
Fri.	play computer games
Sat.	visit grandparents

① Tom played soccer on Monday.
② Tom went swimming on Tuesday.
③ Tom took a math test on Wednesday.
④ Tom played computer games on Friday.
⑤ Tom will visit his grandparents on Saturday.

[14~15] 다음을 읽고 물음에 답하시오.

Jiho: Hi, Minji. What did you do yesterday?
Minji: Hi, Jiho. I went to the amusement park with my family.
Jiho: ⓐ 너는 재미있었니? (have fun)
Minji: Yes. It was great. How about you?
Jiho: Oh, I was really busy.
Minji: What did you do?
Jiho: My classmates and I finished a group project, and after that we did volunteer work.
Minji: Wow, that's great!
Jiho: I was tired but felt good.

14 대화의 내용과 일치하지 <u>않는</u> 것은?

① Minji went to the amusement park yesterday.
② Jiho had a lot of fun with Minji yesterday.
③ Jiho spent time with his classmates yesterday.
④ Jiho helped other people yesterday.
⑤ Jiho felt tired yesterday.

15 서술형

우리말 ⓐ와 뜻이 같도록 괄호 안의 말을 사용하여 영작하시오.

→ _____

16 다음을 부정문으로 바꿔 쓰시오.

(1) I was good at science.
(2) She made a school newspaper.

(1) → _____

(2) → _____

17 어법상 옳은 문장의 개수는?

ⓐ Does she read books on weekends?
ⓑ Tigers and lions doesn't meet in nature.
ⓒ The movie was very boring.
ⓓ Are you go to middle school?
ⓔ Susan didn't had time to have lunch.
ⓕ They made a poster for the contest.

① 2개   ② 3개   ③ 4개
④ 5개   ⑤ 6개

[18~19] 다음은 Jina가 어제 한 일을 적은 것이다. 글을 읽고 물음에 답하시오.

I was very busy yesterday. I ⓐ _____ home at around 3. First, I changed my clothes. And then I cleaned the living room. After that, I ⓑ _____ my dog. After dinner, I ⓒ _____ tired and went to bed.

18 빈칸 ⓐ~ⓒ에 알맞은 말이 순서대로 바르게 나열된 것은?

① come - fed - feel   ② come - feed - felt
③ came - fed - felt   ④ came - feed - felt
⑤ come - feeds - feel

19 서술형

What did Jina do right after she changed her clothes? (5단어)

→ _____

20 [서술형]

그림을 보고 물음에 답하시오.

Q: What is Amy doing now?

A: _____ _____ _____

_____ music.

21 [서술형]

다음을 'an hour ago'가 들어간 문장으로 어법에 맞게 다시 쓰시오.

The monkey breaks a branch and holds it.

→ _____

an hour ago.

22 질문에 대한 응답으로 적절하지 <u>않은</u> 것은?

A: Did you do something good for the environment last weekend?

B: Yes, _____.

① I recycled paper
② I planted some trees
③ I ate up all the food at dinner
④ I threw a can into the Han River
⑤ I picked up some garbage at the park

23 [서술형]

그림을 보고, 과거와 현재를 비교하는 문장을 완성하시오.

Tina ⓐ _____ long hair three months ago, but she ⓑ _____ short hair now.

24 빈칸 ①~⑤에 들어갈 단어의 형태가 알맞지 <u>않은</u> 것은?

May 13th, 2015

It was a bad day today. I ① _____ up late in the morning. I missed my bus, so I ② _____ to school. I ③ _____ late for class. I didn't ④ _____ my book and notebook. I ⑤ _____ ashamed.

① got   ② ran   ③ was
④ brought   ⑤ felt

[고난도]

25 [서술형 심화]

다음은 Josh가 Mary에게 쓴 편지의 일부이다. 어법상 틀린 부분을 네 군데 찾아 문장 기호를 쓰고 바르게 고쳐 쓰시오.

Hi, Mary.
ⓐ I arrived in Korea yesterday. ⓑ My friend Sun-ho picks me up at the airport. ⓒ We went to Insa-dong today. ⓓ I try Bindaeddeok there, and it was good. ⓔ I loved it. ⓕ I buy a beautiful Korean traditional fan there, too. ⓖ I had a good time. ⓗ Did you had a good day, too?

(1) 틀린 기호: _____ → _____
(2) 틀린 기호: _____ → _____
(3) 틀린 기호: _____ → _____
(4) 틀린 기호: _____ → _____

CHAPTER

05

문장의 형식

문장의 5형식

영어의 모든 문장에는 주어와 서술어(동사)가 꼭 필요하다. 하지만 동사 뒤에 오는 말은 동사의 종류에 따라 달라진다. 즉, 동사에 따라 목적어나 보어가 꼭 필요할 수도 있고 아닐 수도 있다.

- 목적어: 서술어가 나타내는 행동의 대상이다. 우리말의 '~을/를'이나 '~에게'에 해당한다. 목적어로 대개 명사, 대명사가 오지만, to부정사구나 동명사구처럼 긴 목적어가 오기도 한다.
- 보어: 주어나 목적어의 상태, 성질에 관해 보충 설명해 주는 말이다.

한눈에 쏙! 문법 Chart

1형식	주어 + 동사 (+ 수식어구)	• The sun rises. • Sally is in her room.
2형식	주어 + 동사 + 보어	She looks tired.
3형식	주어 + 동사 + 목적어	He bought some snacks.
4형식	주어 + 동사 + 간접목적어 + 직접목적어	Jenny gave me this present.
5형식	주어 + 동사 + 목적어 + 목적격 보어	We made her a star.

핵심만 쏙! 문법 Point

Point 01 1형식은 「주어 + 동사」, 2형식은 「주어 + 동사 + 보어」로만 구성돼요!

- **1형식 문장**은 「주어 + 동사」만으로 의미가 완성될 수 있는 문장이다. 보통 형용사구나 부사구와 같은 수식어와 함께 쓴다.
  I wake up at 7. 나는 7시에 일어난다.
  The sun rises in the east. 해는 동쪽에서 뜬다.

- **2형식 문장**은 「주어 + 동사 + 보어」만으로 의미가 완성될 수 있는 문장이다. 보어로는 대개 명사(구)나 형용사(구)가 온다.
  Mr. Kim is *our English teacher*. Mr. Kim은 우리 영어 선생님이다. (Mr. Kim=our English teacher)
  　　　　　주격보어
  My brother is *smart*. 내 남동생은 똑똑하다. (smart가 주어 my brother의 상태를 설명해 줌)
  　　　　　주격보어
  Many leaves turn *red* in autumn. 가을에는 많은 잎들이 빨갛게 변한다. (turn: ~상태로 되다/변하다)
  　　　　　주격보어
  Your dream will come *true*. 너의 꿈은 이루어질 거야. (come: ~되다)
  　　　　　주격보어

Point 02 감각동사 다음에는 형용사가 쓰여요!

- 「주어 + 동사 + 보어」로 이루어진 2형식 문장에는 동사 자리에 '감각동사'가 주로 온다.

- 감각동사 + 형용사:

look / smell / sound / taste / feel	+ 형용사
~하게 보이다/냄새가 나다/들리다/맛이 나다/느껴지다	

You look *sleepy*. 너는 졸려 보인다.
　　　주격보어

The flower smells really *nice*. 그 꽃은 정말 좋은 냄새가 난다.
　　　　　주격보어

The song sounds *wonderful*. 그 노래는 훌륭하게 들린다.
　　　　　주격보어

These grapes taste *sweet and sour*. 이 포도는 새콤달콤한 맛이 난다.
　　　　　주격보어

핵심만 콕! 문법 Check

A 괄호 안에서 알맞은 말을 고르시오.

1 He looked very (happy, happily).

2 The soup smells (good, well).

3 His voice sounded (unusual, unusually).

4 I felt very (nervous, nervously).

B 다음 문장에서 〈주격 보어〉를 찾아 밑줄을 그으시오.

1 The cookies taste bad.

2 I feel happy.

3 His teacher looks kind and gentle.

4 His song sounds beautiful.

C 주어진 문장을 해석하고 몇 형식인지 쓰시오.

1 The wind blew softly.

→ _____ (_____ 형식)

2 My sister goes to high school.

→ _____ (_____ 형식)

3 Jay is my best friend.

→ _____ (_____ 형식)

D 우리말과 뜻이 같도록 괄호 안의 말을 바르게 배열하여 문장을 완성하시오.

1 우리 가족은 서울에 산다. (lives, in, Seoul, my family)

→ _____

2 그의 수업은 재미있다. (class, his, is, interesting)

→ _____

3 Alice는 의사가 되었다. (a doctor, Alice, became)

→ _____

Point 03 3형식 문장은 「주어 + 동사 + 직접목적어」로 구성돼요!

- 3형식 문장은 「주어 + 동사 + 직접목적어」로 이루어진 문장이다.

- **목적어**: 동작의 대상이 되는 말로 문장에서 '무엇을'에 해당한다.
  My sister bought *a new bag*. 우리 언니는 새 가방을 샀다.
              목적어
  I'll order *a slice of pizza*. 나는 피자 한 조각을 주문할 것이다.
          목적어

Point 04 4형식 문장은 「주어 + 동사 + 간접목적어 + 직접목적어」로 구성돼요!

- 4형식 문장은 「주어 + 동사 + 간접목적어 + 직접목적어」로 이루어진 문장이다.
  목적어가 두 개가 온다는 점에서 3형식과는 다르다.

- 문장에서 간접목적어는 '~에게'로, 직접목적어는 '~을, 를'로 해석된다.
  My boyfriend gave *me a ring*. 내 남자친구가 나에게 반지를 주었다.
              간·목 직·목

  Jack bought *his mom a book*. Jack은 그의 엄마에게 책을 사드렸다.
            간·목   직·목

Point 05 4형식 문장은 전치사를 데리고 3형식으로 전환이 가능해요!

- 4형식 문장에서 목적어가 오는 순서를 바꿔 3형식 문장으로 만들 수 있다. 간접목적어와 직접목적어의
  순서를 바꾸고, 간접목적어 앞에 전치사 to, for, of 중에 동사에 맞는 전치사를 하나 쓴다.

전치사 to를 쓰는 동사	bring, give, pass, send, show, teach, tell, write
전치사 for를 쓰는 동사	buy, cook, make, order
전치사 of를 쓰는 동사	ask

My mom wrote <u>me a letter</u>. (4형식) 엄마는 내게 편지를 써줬다.

My mom wrote <u>a letter</u> to <u>me</u>. (3형식)

핵심만 콕! 문법 Check

A 다음 문장에서 동사를 찾아 동그라미 하고, 목적어를 찾아 밑줄을 그으시오.

1 She bought new glasses.

2 Our mom loves us very much.

3 I answered his question.

B 밑줄 친 부분을 어법에 맞게 고쳐 문장 전체를 다시 쓰시오. (단, 4형식 유지)

1 He gave <u>some tips us</u>. (그는 우리에게 약간의 조언을 해주었다.)

→ _____

2 I can <u>teach to him English</u>. (나는 그에게 영어를 가르칠 수 있다.)

→ _____

C 두 문장의 뜻이 같도록 빈칸에 알맞은 말을 쓰시오.

1 I sent him an email already.

→ I _____ him already.

2 Mary made us delicious sandwiches.

→ Mary _____ us.

3 Susie asked him many questions.

→ Susie _____ him.

D 괄호 안의 말을 바르게 배열하여 문장을 완성하시오.

1 그는 우리에게 몇 가지 흥미로운 질문을 했다. (asked, some, questions, interesting, he, of, us)

→ _____

2 지민은 그녀의 남동생에게 책 몇 권을 보냈다. (sent, some, Jimin, to, her, books, brother)

→ _____

핵심만 쏙! 문법 Point

Point 06 5형식 문장은 「주어 + 동사 + 목적어 + 목적격 보어」로 구성돼요!

- 5형식 문장은 「주어 + 동사 + 목적어 + 목적격 보어」로 이루어진 문장이다.

- 목적격 보어는 목적어를 보충 설명해 주는 말로 명사(구)나 형용사(구)가 올 수 있다.
  We call *our dog Lucky*. 우리는 우리 강아지를 Lucky라 불렀다.
  　　　　목적어　목·보

  The news made *them angry*. 그 소식은 그들을 화나게 만들었다.
  　　　　　　목적어　목·보

  Mrs. White always keeps *her desk clean*. Mrs. White는 그녀의 책상을 항상 깨끗하게 한다.
  　　　　　　　　목적어　　목·보

Point 07 미래지향적 동사들은 목적격 보어로 to부정사를 사용해요!

- 목적어를 보충해 주는 목적격 보어로 to부정사가 쓰이기도 한다.

- 목적격 보어로 to부정사를 취하는 동사에는 want, ask, tell, allow, expect, order 등이 있다.
  I want him to forget her. 나는 그가 그녀를 잊었으면 한다.
  He told her not to be late again. 그는 그녀에게 다시 늦지 말라고 이야기 했다.
  My mom allowed me to use the computer for an hour.
  엄마는 내가 한 시간 동안 컴퓨터를 사용할 수 있도록 허락해 주셨다.

Point 08 사역동사와 지각동사는 목적격 보어로 동사원형을 사용해요!

- **사역동사의 목적격 보어**: 목적어와 목적격 보어의 관계가 능동일 때는 동사원형이, 수동일 때는 과거분사가 온다.
  Mr. Kim made us study harder. Mr. Kim은 우리가 공부를 더 열심히 하도록 만들었다. (능동: 동사원형)
  I had my ring stolen. 나는 내 반지를 도둑맞았다. (수동: 과거분사)

- **지각동사의 목적격 보어**: 목적어와 목적격 보어의 관계가 능동일 때 보통 동사원형이 오지만, 동작이 진행 중임을 강조할 때 '동사원형 + ing(현재분사)'가 올 수도 있다. 목적어와 목적격 보어의 관계가 수동이면 과거분사가 온다.
  I saw them talk to each other. 나는 그들이 서로 이야기하는 것을 보았다. (능동: 동사원형)
  I saw them talking to each other. 나는 그들이 서로 이야기하고 있는 것을 보았다. (능동이며 진행 강조: 현재분사)
  We heard him called Andrew. 우리는 그가 Andrew라고 불리는 것을 들었다. (수동: 과거분사)

- **help의 목적격 보어**: 'to부정사' 또는 '원형부정사(동사원형)' 둘 다 올 수 있다.
  Sang-ho helped us (to) find the way. 상호는 우리가 길을 찾는 것을 도와줬다.

핵심만 콕! 문법 Check

A 괄호 안에서 알맞은 말을 고르시오.

1 My mom made me (clean, to clean) my room.

2 I saw them (fight, fought) on the street.

3 He helped us (carrying, to carry) the bag.

4 The doctor had him (eat, eating) fewer calories.

B 밑줄 친 부분을 어법에 맞도록 고쳐 문장을 다시 쓰시오.

1 My mom wouldn't let us <u>to play</u> computer games.

→ _____

2 Mr. Johnson made us <u>cleaned</u> the hall.

→ _____

3 I had my son <u>did</u> his homework.

→ _____

C 밑줄 친 부분에 유의하여 우리말로 해석하시오.

1 I <u>want</u> you <u>to be happy all the time</u>.

→ _____

2 We didn't <u>expect</u> him <u>to finish it on time</u>.

→ _____

3 My mom <u>told</u> me <u>to wash the dishes</u>.

→ _____

D 괄호 안의 말을 바르게 배열하여 문장을 완성하시오.

1 그는 우리가 들어오게 하지 않았다. (didn't, let, he, us, come in)

→ _____

2 우리는 그들이 미소 짓는 것을 보았다. (saw, them, we, smiling)

→ _____

3 그들은 내가 그 노래를 부르는 것을 들었다. (they, heard, me, sing, the song)

→ _____

내신 만점! 실전 기출

[1~2] 빈칸에 알맞지 <u>않은</u> 것을 고르시오.

01

> John's idea sounds _____.

① great
② wonderfully
③ funny
④ interesting
⑤ fantastic

02

> Ms. Kim felt _____.

① sad   ② lonely   ③ happy
④ angry   ⑤ sleep

03 서술형

괄호 안의 말을 재배열하여 의문문을 완성하시오.

> 너는 그녀에게 케이크를 사 줄 수 있니?
> (you, can, buy, her, a cake)

→ _____

04 서술형

어법상 틀린 곳을 한 군데 찾아 그 기호를 쓰고, 문장 전체를 바르게 고쳐 쓰시오.

> ⓐ The apple pie ⓑ smells ⓒ deliciously.

→ 기호: _____

→ _____

05 어법상 <u>틀린</u> 문장을 고르시오.

① His answer made me sad.
② We call him Super Mario.
③ I saw my mom to dance.
④ Mr. Kim made them study hard.
⑤ She will help us to clean the room.

06 문장의 형식이 <u>다른</u> 하나를 고르시오.

① The work made us tired.
② My mom had me clean the room.
③ Julie helped him do his homework.
④ John wants to go to the concert.
⑤ The children call their puppy Genie.

07 빈칸에 알맞은 말을 고르시오.

> All of his friends looked _____.

① lovely   ② happily   ③ excitedly
④ nicely   ⑤ funnily

08 빈칸에 알맞지 <u>않은</u> 것은?

> Mr. Kim _____ the students not to make noise in the library.

① told   ② had   ③ asked
④ wanted   ⑤ warned

09 어법상 옳은 문장을 <u>모두</u> 고르면?

① The people in the office all look friendly.
② I want him do the dishes this time.
③ Everyone elected him president.
④ She always makes me happily.
⑤ His father saw him to sing.

10 서술형

괄호 안의 말을 활용하여 문장을 완성하시오.

그녀의 아버지께서는 건강해 보이셨다.

→ _____

_____ (look, healthy)

신유형

11 주어진 단어들을 배열하여 문장을 만들 때, 앞에서 <u>네 번째</u> 올 단어는?

(They, alone, her, heard, sing)

① They   ② alone   ③ her
④ heard   ⑤ sing

12 빈칸에 알맞지 <u>않은</u> 것은?

Mr. Choi _____ us help him.

① made   ② had   ③ let
④ got   ⑤ helped

13 서술형

두 문장의 뜻이 같도록 빈칸에 알맞은 말을 쓰시오.

Sang-ho gave Gloria beautiful earrings.

→ Sang-ho gave _____ _____
_____ Gloria.

14 밑줄 친 부분이 어법상 옳지 <u>않은</u> 것을 고르시오.

Jimin <u>gave</u> <u>to him</u> <u>a love letter</u> yesterday.
         ①   ②   ③
He looked <u>very</u> <u>surprised</u>.
              ④   ⑤

15 우리말을 영어로 바르게 옮긴 것을 고르시오.

나는 그가 훌륭한 음악인이라고 생각한다.

① I consider to him a great musician.
② I consider of him a great musician.
③ I consider him a great musician.
④ I consider a great musician of him.
⑤ I consider him been a great musician.

16 빈칸에 알맞은 말이 순서대로 나열된 것은?

A: The food smells ⓐ _____.
   I feel ⓑ _____.
B: I am hungry, too.
   But we have to wait until Dad comes.

① nice — hunger
② nice – hungrily
③ nicely – hungrily
④ nicely – hungry
⑤ nice – hungry

17 서술형

우리말과 일치하도록 완전한 영어 문장으로 쓰시오.
(단, 조건을 충족하시오.)

┌─ 조건 ─────────────────────┐
1. 어휘: clean, keep, should를 포함할 것.
2. 6단어로 이루어진 완전한 문장으로 쓸 것.
└──────────────────────────┘

우리는 우리의 책상들을 깨끗하게 유지해야 한다.

→ _____

고난도

18 서술형

〈보기〉처럼 두 문장을 한 문장으로 연결하여 다시 쓰시오.

┌─ 조건 ─────────────────────┐
They sang together. We heard them.
→ We heard them sing together.
└──────────────────────────┘

He crossed the street. I saw him.

→ _____

19 빈칸에 공통으로 알맞은 말은?

- Our teacher _____ us wear a uniform.
- The classical music _____ me feel calm.

① taught   ② told   ③ asked
④ ordered   ⑤ made

20 빈칸에 알맞은 말이 나머지와 다른 하나는?

① Can you send an email _____ him?
② Mom likes to write letters _____ me.
③ Please pass the salt _____ me.
④ Will she give a present _____ us?
⑤ He bought a nice present _____ them.

21 두 문장의 뜻이 같도록 빈칸에 알맞은 말이 순서대로 나열된 것은?

(1) Mom made us a huge cake.
  = Mom made a huge cake ⓐ _____ us.
(2) The reporter asked me a lot of questions.
  = The reporter asked a lot of questions ⓑ _____ me.

① at, by   ② at, for   ③ for, by
④ for, of   ⑤ for, about

22 서술형

우리말과 뜻이 같도록 문장을 완성하시오.

장시간의 기다림이 그들을 피곤하게 만들었다.

→ Long hours of waiting _____
_____ _____.

23 서술형

괄호 안의 말을 활용하여 ⓐ의 우리말을 영어로 영작하시오.
(단, 4형식 문장으로 쓸 것)

M: Hey. How did you spend your birthday?
W: Our family got together and had a birthday party. It was a lot of fun.
M: Oh. Sounds like you had a good time. What did you get for birthday presents?
W: ⓐ 나의 부모님께서 나에게 좋은 시계를 주셨어. (parents, gave, watch, a, nice)
M: Oh, is it the one you're wearing now?
W: Yes, it is. I really like it.

→ _____
_____

24 서술형

밑줄 친 부분이 어법상 틀린 문장을 모두 찾아 그 기호를 쓰고, 바르게 고쳐 쓰시오. (단, 문장의 형식은 유지)

(a) His idea <u>sounds great</u>.

(b) She <u>gave us a few pieces of chocolate</u>.

(c) I will <u>make a cake to him</u>.

(d) Everyone <u>calls her an angel</u>.

(e) I <u>want you come</u> with me.

(f) You <u>look lovely</u> without your glasses.

(g) He <u>sent to me a text message</u> last night.

(h) The students <u>felt the ground shake</u>.

(i) I <u>showed my new bike to the boy</u>.

(j) My mom didn't <u>let me playing computer games</u>.

(k) My English teacher <u>advised me read</u> the book.

(기호):   (수정된 어구)

→ _____ : _____

→ _____ : _____

→ _____ : _____

→ _____ : _____

→ _____ : _____

고난도

25 서술형 심화

다음은 Julie의 생일에 Julie의 가족들이 그녀에게 해준 일을 적은 표이다. 〈보기〉와 같이 문장을 완성하시오.

Who	What
Mom	make cake
Dad	buy a new bag
Sister	write a letter

보기

Mom made Julie a cake.
→ Mom made a cake for Julie.

(1) Dad _____ _____ _____ _____ bag.

→ Dad _____ _____ _____ _____ _____ _____.

(2) Julie's sister _____ _____ a letter.

→ Julie's sister _____ _____ _____ _____ _____.

CHAPTER

06

to 부정사와 동명사

to부정사

「to + 동사원형」의 형태로 동사의 성질을 가진 채로 문장 안에서 명사, 형용사, 부사의 역할을 한다.

동명사

「동사원형-ing」의 형태로 동사의 성질을 가진 채로 문장 안에서 명사의 역할을 한다.

• to부정사와 동명사의 역할

		I like books.
to부정사	명사 역할	I like **to read** books.
	형용사 역할	I borrowed books **to read**.
	부사 역할	I finished my homework early **to read the book**.
동명사	명사 역할	I like **reading** books.

한눈에 쏙! 문법 Chart

부정사	명사적 용법	1. 주어, 보어, 목적어로 쓰인다. 2. 「의문사 + to부정사」
	형용사적 용법	명사 뒤에서 수식해 준다.
	부사적 용법	목적(~하기 위해), 감정의 원인(~해서), 판단의 근거(~하다니), 결과(~해서 그 결과 ~하다)
	to부정사를 목적어로 취하는 동사	want, ask, decide, expect, learn, hope, plan, promise 등의 미래와 관련된 의미를 가지는 동사들
동명사	명사 역할	1. 문장의 주어, 보어, 목적어로 쓰인다. 2. 전치사의 목적어로 쓰인다. (전치사 뒤에는 to부정사가 오지 못한다.)
	동명사를 목적어로 취하는 동사	mind, enjoy, give up, avoid, finish, escape, practice, stop
to부정사와 동명사가 목적어로 올 때 뜻이 달라지는 동사들		forget/remember + to부정사: ~할 것을 잊다/기억하다 forget/remember + 동명사: ~한 것을 잊다/기억하다 try + to부정사: ~하려고 노력하다 try + 동명사: 시험 삼아 ~해 보다 stop + to부정사: ~하기 위해 멈추다 stop + 동명사: ~을 그만두다

핵심만 쏙! 문법 Point

Point 01 to부정사는 문장에서 명사처럼 주어, 보어, 목적어로 쓰여요!

- to부정사는 「to + 동사원형」의 형태로 문장에서 명사, 형용사, 부사의 역할을 한다.

- **to부정사의 명사적 용법:** to부정사가 명사처럼 쓰일 때는 문장에서 주어, 목적어, 보어 역할을 하며, '~하기, ~하는 것'으로 해석된다. to부정사가 주어로 쓰인 경우, 대부분 주어 자리에 가주어 it을 쓰고 to부정사를 뒤로 보낸다.

주어 역할	To master English is my goal. 영어를 숙달하는 것이 나의 목표이다. → It is my goal to master English.
보어 역할	My dream is to enter Harvard University. 나의 꿈은 하버드대학에 입학하는 것이다.
목적어 역할	I want to travel the world in the future. 나는 장래에 세계 여행하기를 원한다.

- **to부정사를 목적어로 취하는 동사:** want, ask, decide, expect, learn, hope, plan, promise 등의 미래와 관련된 의미를 가지는 동사들이다.
  Giho planned to visit his cousin in New York. 기호는 뉴욕에 있는 그의 사촌을 방문하기로 계획했다.
  My father promised to stop smoking. 아빠는 금연하기로 약속하셨다.

- **to부정사의 부정:** 「not + to부정사」로 쓴다.
  The mouse tried not to wake up the lion. 쥐는 사자를 깨우지 않으려고 노력했다.

Point 02 「의문사 + to부정사」는 문장 안에서 명사 역할로 쓰여요!

- 「의문사 + to부정사」는 문장 안에서 명사 역할을 하며, 주로 목적어로 쓰인다.

how + to부정사: 어떻게 ~할지, ~하는 방법	what + to부정사: 무엇을 ~할지
when + to부정사: 언제 ~할지	where + to부정사: 어디로 ~할지
who(m) + to부정사: 누구를 ~할지	

Please tell me how to copy this file. 이 파일을 어떻게 복사하는지 알려주세요.
He didn't know what to do next. 그는 그 다음에 무엇을 해야 할지 몰랐다.

핵심만 콕! 문법 Check

A 괄호 안에서 알맞은 말을 고르시오.

1 His job is (write, to write) songs.

2 (Swim, To swim) at sea is not easy.

3 Do you want (be, to be) a fashion designer?

4 She decided (to not visit, not to visit) her parents' house today.

B 빈칸에 알맞은 말을 〈보기〉에서 골라 알맞은 형태로 쓰시오.

> 보기
>
> learn   travel   wake up   watch   be   teach

1 그는 비행사가 되기로 결심했다.

→ He decided _____ a pilot.

2 축구 경기를 보는 것은 재미있다.

→ It is fun _____ soccer games.

3 엄마가 나에게 아기를 깨우지 말라고 말씀하셨다.

→ Mom told me _____ the baby.

C 우리말과 뜻이 같도록 알맞은 의문사와 괄호 안의 단어를 활용하여 빈칸에 알맞은 말을 쓰시오

1 그는 그것을 사기 위해 어디로 가야 할지 생각했다.

→ He thought about _____ to buy it. (go)

2 그녀는 무엇을 고를지 잠시 망설였다.

→ She wondered _____ for a moment. (choose)

3 그는 그 기계를 어떻게 사용하는지 보여주었다.

→ He showed me _____ the machine. (use)

4 언제 멈춰야 하는지 말씀해 주세요.

→ Please tell me _____. (stop)

D 우리말과 뜻이 같도록 괄호 안의 말을 바르게 배열하여 문장을 완성하시오.

1 나는 그것을 어디에 숨겨야 할지 몰랐다. (where, I, hide, know, to, it, didn't)

→ _____

2 도서관으로 가는 방법을 제게 말해 주세요. (to, get, to, library, the, how, tell, me)

→ Please _____

핵심만 쏙! 문법 Point

Point 03 to부정사가 명사 뒤에서 명사를 꾸며 주면 형용사적 용법이에요!

- **to부정사의 형용사적 용법**: to부정사는 명사 뒤에서 형용사처럼 명사를 꾸며줄 수 있으며, '~할, ~해야 할'로 해석한다.
  Sujin wants **a book** to read. 수진이는 읽을 책을 원한다.
  Jake brought **something** to drink. Jake는 마실 것을 가져왔다.

- to부정사의 수식을 받는 명사가 to부정사 속의 동사에 이어지는 전치사의 목적어인 경우 「명사 + to부정사 + 전치사」의 형태로 쓴다.
  You write with **a pen**. → Do you need **a pen** to write with? 너는 쓸 펜이 필요하니?
  You sit on **a chair**. → Shall I give you **a chair** to sit on? 앉을 의자를 드릴까요?
  You live in **a house**. → Let's find **a house** to live in. 살 집을 찾아 보자.

Point 04 to부정사가 '목적, 감정의 원인, 판단의 근거, 결과'로 해석되면 부사적 용법이에요!

- **to부정사의 부사적 용법**: 문장에서 부사 역할을 하며 목적, 감정의 원인, 판단의 근거, 결과 등의 의미를 나타낸다.

목적	~하기 위해	She worked in a factory to help her family. 그녀는 가족을 도와주기 위해 공장에서 일했다.
감정의 원인	~해서	I am glad to see you. 너를 만나서 기쁘다.
판단의 근거	~하다니	It was kind of you to help me. 나를 도와주다니 너 참 친절하구나.
결과	~해서 그 결과 ~하다	She grew up to be a pianist. 그녀는 자라서 피아니스트가 되었다.

핵심만 콕! 문법 Check

A 괄호 안에서 알맞은 말을 고르시오.

1 Seoul has many places (visit, to visit).
2 The old lady needs a chair (to sit, to sit on).
3 He didn't have a chance (meet, to meet) her.
4 She asked for some paper (to write, to write on).
5 I want to buy a game (to play, to play with)
6 They were looking for an apartment (to live, to live in).

B 밑줄 친 부분을 어법에 맞게 고쳐 쓰시오. (필요하면 전치사를 추가하여 쓰시오.)

1 I have homework <u>finish</u>.　　→　_____
2 I have something <u>tell</u> you.　　→　_____
3 Please lend me a pen <u>write</u>.　　→　_____
4 She wants to make friends <u>play</u>.　　→　_____
5 Jina bought a game <u>play</u>.　　→　_____
6 Mike needs something <u>eat</u>.　　→　_____

C 우리말과 뜻이 같도록 괄호 안의 말을 바르게 배열하여 문장을 완성하시오.

1 너는 할 일이 있니? (do, anything, to)
→ Do you have _____?

2 이제 가야 할 시간이다. (go, time, to)
→ It's _____ now.

3 요즘 볼 만한 영화가 있니? (movies, watch, good, to, any)
→ Are there _____ these days?

D 〈보기〉와 같이 두 문장을 한 문장으로 만드시오.

> 보기
> Mina listens to English songs. + She wants to practice English.
> → Mina listens to English songs <u>to practice</u> English.

1 He grew up. + He became a doctor.
→ He grew up _____ a doctor.

2 Mary was really happy. + She got an A.
→ Mary was really happy _____ an A.

핵심만 쏙! 문법 Point

Point 05 동명사는 문장에서 명사처럼 주어, 보어, 목적어로 쓰여요!

■ **동명사:** 「동사원형-ing」의 형태로 문장에서 명사처럼 주어, 보어, 목적어의 역할을 하며, '하기' 또는 '하는 것'으로 해석된다.

> • run (달리다) → running (달리기)
> • learn English (영어를 배우다) → learning English (영어를 배우기)

Do you like painting? 너는 그림 그리기를 좋아하니?

cf. 현재분사: '~하고 있는'으로 해석되면, 동명사가 아니라 '현재분사'이다.
He **is** painting a tree. 그는 나무를 그리고 있는 중이다. (이 문장의 painting: 현재분사)

■ **동명사의 부정:** 「not[never] + 동사원형-ing」으로 쓴다.
She felt sorry for not coming on time. 그녀는 제시간에 오지 못한 것에 대해 미안했다.

Point 06 동명사가 목적어로 오는 동사: <u>m</u>ind, <u>e</u>njoy, <u>g</u>ive up, <u>a</u>void, <u>f</u>inish, <u>e</u>scape, <u>s</u>top → megafes(메가패스)!

■ **타동사의 목적어로 쓰인 동명사:** '~하는 것을'로 해석한다. 동명사를 목적어로 취하는 동사로는 mind, enjoy, give up, avoid, finish, escape, practice, stop 등이 있다.
She **enjoyed** listening to music. 그녀는 음악 듣는 것을 즐겼다.
Do you **mind** opening the window? 창문을 열어도 될까요?

■ **동사가 전치사의 목적어로 올 때:** 동명사의 형태인 「동사원형-ing」로 와야 한다.
He is good **at** making jokes. 그는 농담을 잘한다.
I am interested **in** helping poor children. 나는 불쌍한 어린이들을 돕는 것에 관심이 있다.

핵심만 콕! 문법 Check

A 괄호 안의 말을 알맞은 형태로 바꾸어 빈칸에 쓰시오

1 Don't give up _____ to solve the riddle. (try)

2 _____ homework is helpful for students. (do)

3 He was afraid of _____ the test. (pass, not)

4 Emily finished _____ her essay. (write)

5 Father promised _____ me a new bike. (buy)

6 Have you decided _____ the speaking contest? (enter)

B 〈보기〉와 같이 밑줄 친 부분을 우리말로 해석하고, 현재분사인지 동명사인지 쓰시오.

> 보기
> (a) His hobby is <u>collecting</u> stamps.　　　　→ <u>수집하기 (동명사)</u>
> (b) He is <u>collecting</u> stamps from envelopes.　→ <u>모으고 있는 중인 (현재분사)</u>

1 (a) She enjoys <u>listening</u> to music.　　　　→ _____

  (b) She is <u>listening</u> to music.　　　　　→ _____

2 (a) Her dream is <u>dancing</u> on stage.　　　→ _____

  (b) She is <u>dancing</u> on stage now.　　　→ _____

C 우리말과 뜻이 같도록 괄호 안의 말을 바르게 배열하여 문장을 완성하시오.

1 자전거를 타는 것은 재미있다. (is, a bike, fun, riding)

→ _____

2 그녀의 취미는 피아노를 연주하는 것이다. (playing, hobby, the piano, is, her)

→ _____

3 우리는 바다에 쓰레기를 버리는 것을 그만해야 한다. (stop, throwing, garbage)

→ _____

D 우리말과 뜻이 같도록 괄호 안의 말을 활용하여 문장을 완성하시오.

1 나는 음악에 맞춰 춤을 잘 춘다. (good, dance)

→ I am _____ _____ _____ to music.

2 우리는 즐겁게 양로원의 어르신들을 도와드렸다. (enjoy, help)

→ We _____ _____ the elderly people in the nursing home.

Point 07 forget, remember, try, stop은 뒤에 to부정사나 동명사가 올 때 뜻이 달라져요!

- to부정사와 동명사를 의미 차이 없이 모두 목적어로 취하는 동사는 start, begin, like, love, continue 등이 있다.
  She **likes** to take care of children. = She **likes** taking care of children.

- to부정사와 동명사가 목적어로 올 때 뜻이 달라지는 동사는 다음과 같다.

forget	+ to부정사: (미래) ~할 것을 잊다	Don't forget to water the flower. 꽃에 물 주는 것을 잊지마.
	+ 동명사: (과거) ~한 것을 잊다	**She forgot** watering **the flower.** 그녀는 꽃에 물 준 것을 잊었다.
remember	+ to부정사: (미래) ~할 것을 기억하다	Remember to call her tomorrow. 내일 그녀에게 전화해야 하는 것을 기억해.
	+ 동명사: (과거) ~한 것을 기억하다	He remembered meeting her. 그는 그녀를 만났던 것을 기억한다.
try	+ to부정사: ~하려고 노력하다	The boy tried to climb the tree. 소년은 나무에 올라가려고 애썼다.
	+ 동명사: 시험 삼아 ~해 보다	The boy tried climbing the tree. 그는 시험 삼아 나무에 올라가 보았다.
stop	+ to부정사: ~하기 위해 멈추다 (부정사의 부사적 용법)	People stopped to listen to the music. 사람들은 음악을 듣기 위해 멈췄다.
	+ 동명사: ~하는 것을 멈추다 (목적어로 쓰인 동명사)	They stopped listening to the music. 그들은 음악 듣는 것을 멈추었다.

Point 08 동명사를 목적어로 취하는 관용표현 이에요!

- 동명사를 이용한 관용적 표현은 다음과 같다.

go ~ing	~하러 가다	He **went** hiking yesterday. 그는 어제 하이킹을 갔다.
How[What] about ~ing?	~하는 게 어때?	**How[What] about** watching TV? TV 보는 것은 어때?
be good at ~ing	~을 잘하다	She **is good at** cooking. 그녀는 요리를 잘한다.
spend + (시간, 돈) + ~ing	~하는 데 (시간, 돈)을 쓰다	He **spent a lot of** time playing games. 그는 게임하는 데 많은 시간을 보냈다.
look forward to ~ing	~할 것을 고대하다	I **look forward to** seeing you soon. 곧 만나기를 고대할게.

핵심만 콕! 문법 Check

A 두 문장의 뜻이 같도록 괄호 안에서 알맞은 말을 고르시오.

1 He likes to swim in the river.

= He likes (swim, swimming) in the river.

2 They started to play music.

= They started (play, playing) music.

B 괄호 안에서 알맞은 말을 고르시오.

1 How about (to go, going) to a movie?

2 Tom wants (to return, returning) the books to the library.

3 Did you mind (to be, being) away from home for so long?

4 We are looking forward to (meet, meeting) you.

C 우리말과 뜻이 같도록 괄호 안의 말을 활용하여 문장을 완성하시오

1 그녀는 드레스를 한 번 입어 보았다. (put on)

→ She tried _____ the dress.

2 그녀는 꽃의 냄새를 맡기 위해 멈췄다. (smell)

→ She stopped _____ the flowers.

3 아빠는 이번 주 토요일에 나와 함께 낚시를 가기로 약속했다. (fish)

→ Dad promised to go _____ with me this Saturday.

D 우리말과 뜻이 같도록 괄호 안의 말을 바르게 배열하여 문장을 완성하시오.

1 도서관에서 함께 공부하는 게 어때? (study, about, what)

→ _____ _____ _____ in the library together?

2 그는 수학 문제를 푸는 데 하루 종일 시간을 보냈다. (solve, spent, day, the, whole)

→ He _____ _____ _____ _____ _____ math problems.

3 민호는 중국어를 배우기로 결심했다. (learn, decided, to)

→ Minho _____ _____ _____ Chinese.

4 우리는 당신의 쇼를 다시 보게 될 것을 고대하고 있습니다. (watching, looking, to, forward)

→ We are _____ _____ _____ _____ your show again.

5 교과서를 가져 오는 것을 잊지 마세요. (bring, forget, don't, to)

→ _____ _____ _____ _____ your textbooks.

[1~3] 빈칸에 알맞은 것을 고르시오.

01

Tina enjoys _____ care of babies.

① take ② takes ③ taking
④ to take ⑤ took

02

He wants _____ our club.

① join ② joins ③ joining
④ to join ⑤ joined

03

We go to the school library _____ because there are so many interesting books there.

① having lunch
② buy books
③ play games
④ to read books
⑤ to practice soccer

04 빈칸에 알맞지 않은 것은?

She _____ to play the flute at the school contest.

① gave up ② planned
③ decided ④ began
⑤ hoped

05 서술형

〈보기〉처럼, 가주어 it을 사용하여 문장을 다시 쓰시오.

┌─ 보기 ─┐
To learn English requires a lot of practice.

→ It requires a lot of practice to learn English.

To get an A⁺ is not easy.

→ _____

06 밑줄 친 부분의 쓰임이 나머지와 다른 하나는?

① I finished writing my report.
② His hobby is building furniture.
③ Eating rice with a fork looks very strange.
④ We really enjoyed playing soccer the other day.
⑤ They are playing the popular opera "The Marriage of Figaro."

07 밑줄 친 부분의 용법이 나머지와 다른 하나는?

① His favorite activity is to play basketball.
② He loves to take pictures of people.
③ They went there to do volunteer work.
④ We like to climb mountains on weekends.
⑤ She wanted to help poor children in Africa.

08 밑줄 친 부분이 어법상 올바른 것은?

① I am going to late for school.
② Do you love walking with your dog?
③ Mary will learns Spanish this semester.
④ They want play basketball in the afternoon.
⑤ He likes go swimming on hot summer days.

09 서술형

그림을 보고 대화문을 완성하시오. (단, to부정사를 활용)

Q: Why did they go to the field?

A: They went there _____

_____. (3단어)

 최다빈출

[10~12] 어법상 어색한 것을 고르시오.

10

① Stop smoking! It's a bad habit.

② She gave up looking for her lost dog.

③ Please tell me how to take a photo.

④ You have to finish doing your homework.

⑤ We really enjoyed to watch the movie last weekend.

11

① He called me to ask questions.

② Ann doesn't like to eat fast food.

③ We go to school to learn many things.

④ Yumi stopped eating sweets to lose weight.

⑤ Remember buying some snacks tomorrow.

12

① She wants a friend to play.

② They need a house to live in.

③ Is there anybody to help me?

④ Do you want something to drink?

⑤ Please give me a pen to write with.

13 짝지어진 두 문장의 의미가 같지 않은 것은?

① I forgot to water the flower.

= I forgot watering the flower.

② They love to play soccer.

= They love playing soccer.

③ Mom likes to take photos.

= Mom likes taking photos.

④ You are good at cooking.

= You cook really well.

⑤ I am going to go to Busan today.

= I will go to Busan today.

14 밑줄 친 부분의 용법이 같은 것들로만 묶인 것은?

ⓐ Do you want to join the club?

ⓑ The guide always walks in front to lead people.

ⓒ We are here to protect this city from the enemy.

ⓓ My dream is to become a great inventor.

ⓔ I turned off the light to go to bed.

ⓕ Would you like something to eat?

① ⓐ, ⓒ, ⓔ　　② ⓑ, ⓒ, ⓔ　　③ ⓐ, ⓓ, ⓕ

④ ⓑ, ⓓ, ⓕ　　⑤ ⓒ, ⓔ, ⓕ

15 ⓐ~ⓒ에 어법상 알맞은 말이 순서대로 나열된 것은?

Dear Nanuri Club members,

Thank you for ⓐ (visit, visiting) our hospital. All the children here enjoyed ⓑ (to have, having) you. Singing and dancing with you was a lot of fun. We all want ⓒ (thank, to thank) you.

① visit, to have, thank

② visiting, having, to thank

③ visit, having, to thank

④ visiting, having, thank

⑤ visit, to have, to thank

16 밑줄 친 ⓐ~ⓔ 중 어법상 옳지 <u>않은</u> 것을 <u>모두</u> 고르면?

Last weekend, I planned ⓐ <u>watching</u> a movie with my friend at 2 o'clock. So I finished ⓑ <u>doing</u> my homework early and left home. I expected ⓒ <u>to meet</u> my friend in front of the subway station, but she was not there. I called her several times, but she didn't answer. I kept ⓓ <u>to wait</u> for her for 30 minutes. After that, I gave up ⓔ <u>waiting</u> for her. I got really upset.

① ⓐ, ⓒ   ② ⓐ, ⓓ   ③ ⓐ, ⓔ
④ ⓑ, ⓓ   ⑤ ⓑ, ⓔ

17 서술형

괄호 안의 단어를 활용하여 빈칸을 완성하시오. (3단어)

A: I want to make a copy of this. Would you help me?
B: OK. I will show you _____ _____ _____ this copy machine. (use)
First, put the document on the glass.
Then, press the COPY button.
A: That's easy! Thank you so much.

18 신유형

ⓐ~ⓔ의 우리말 해석이 <u>어색한</u> 것은?

Once upon a time, there was a squirrel. He ⓐ <u>was looking for food</u>. Then he found an acorn and ⓑ <u>stopped to pick it up</u>. It was delicious. Then he heard some noise and ⓒ <u>stopped eating</u>. Everything was quiet. When he ⓓ <u>started eating again</u>, he heard the sound again. It was a roaring sound. He ⓔ <u>remembered hearing</u> about a wood monster.

*acorn: 도토리, roaring: 으르렁거리는

① ⓐ: 먹이를 찾고 있었다   ② ⓑ: 줍는 것을 멈췄다
③ ⓒ: 먹는 것을 멈췄다   ④ ⓓ: 다시 먹기 시작했다
⑤ ⓔ: 들었던 것을 기억했다

19 서술형

〈보기〉와 같이 to부정사를 활용하여 두 문장을 한 문장으로 만드시오.

보기
Cindy wants to buy some pencils.
+ She is going to the store.
→ Cindy is going to the store to buy some pencils.

Jina wants to see the Eiffel Tower.
+ She is going to go to Paris next week.
→ _____
_____

20 서술형

괄호 안의 말을 활용하여 문장을 완성하시오.
(필요하면 형태를 바꾸시오.)

(1) 그는 장갑을 한 번 껴보았다. (put on)
→ He tried _____ the gloves.
(2) 그녀는 꽃을 사기 위해 멈추었다. (buy)
→ She stopped _____ flowers.

21 서술형

다음은 진수가 좋아하거나 싫어하는 활동을 나타낸 표이다. 표와 내용이 일치하도록 빈칸에 알맞은 말을 쓰시오.

(×: 싫어함, ○: 좋아함)

Activity	Like or Dislike
Read a book	×
Ride a bike	○
Play soccer	○

→ Jinsu doesn't like to read books, but he enjoys _____ a bike. He also loves _____ soccer.

[22~23] 괄호 안의 말을 활용하여 우리말을 영어로 바꿔 쓰시오. (필요하면 형태를 바꾸시오.)

22 서술형

A: You know we are going to visit the modern painting exhibition tomorrow morning, right?
B: Right. I remember.
A: Don't be late. 자기 전에 알람 시계를 설정하는 것을 잊지 마! (not, set, your alarm, forget)

→ _____

before you go to bed.

23 서술형

A: Tom, why don't we go outside to do something?
스포츠 하기에 좋은 날씨야. (the weather, play, is, for, good, sports)
B: That's a good idea. Let's go.

→ _____

24 서술형

우리말과 뜻이 같도록 괄호 안의 말을 활용하여 문장을 완성하시오.

A: Uh-oh, I left my USB in the library.
B: _____ (what, call)
(도서관 분실물 보관소에 전화해 보는 게 어때?)
A: Okay, I will.

→ _____

the Lost and Found of the library?

25 서술형 심화

Find THREE grammatical errors, and correct them.

Attention, please. This is Amy, your guide for today. We are going to visit the Korean Folk Village. I am glad showing it to you. The Korean Folk Village is a great place learning about Korean culture. You will see traditional Korean houses and clothes there. You can also try to play some traditional Korean games, too. It'll be a lot of fun. Now let's go!

(1) _____ → _____
(2) _____ → _____
(3) _____ → _____

CHAPTER

07

형용사와 부사

형용사

형용사는 사람이나 사물의 성질, 상태, 특징 등을 나타내는 말이다. 즉, '예쁜(pretty), 똑똑한(smart), 좋은(nice)' 등과 같이 명사를 꾸며주는 역할을 한다.

부사

부사는 동작이나 상태를 구체적으로 설명하는 말이다. 즉, '빨리(fast), 친절하게(kindly), 정말로(really)' 등과 같이, 동사, 형용사, 다른 부사, 또는 문장 전체를 꾸며 주는 역할을 한다. 부사는 대개 형용사에 -ly를 붙인 형태가 많지만, 그렇지 않은 경우도 있다.

한눈에 쏙! 문법 Chart

형용사	명사 수식	I have a purple pen.
	보어	My pen is purple.
부사	동사 수식	The bear moves slowly.
	부사나 형용사 수식	The boy runs very quickly.
	문장 수식	Luckily, she's safe now.

핵심만 쏙! 문법 Point

Point 01 형용사는 명사를 꾸며주거나(한정적용법), 보어의 역할(서술적 용법)로 쓰여요!

Kevin is a <u>smart</u> student. Kevin은 똑똑한 학생이다.

Can I get *something* <u>cold</u> to drink? 차가운 마실 것을 얻을 수 있을까요?

He is <u>honest and faithful</u>. 그는 정직하고 진실하다. (주어 he를 보충 설명)
　　　　주격보어

I found this book <u>interesting</u>. 나는 이 책이 재미있다는 것을 알았다. (목적어 this book을 보충 설명)
　　　　　　　　　　목적격보어

Point 02 부사는 동사, 형용사, 다른 부사 또는 문장 전체를 꾸며주는 역할로 쓰여요!

■ 부사는 동사, 형용사, 다른 부사 또는 문장 전체를 꾸며주는 역할을 한다.
Minsu <u>studies</u> <u>hard</u>. 민수는 열심히 공부한다. (동사 수식)

This movie is <u>so</u> <u>sad</u>. 이 영화는 매우 슬프다. (형용사 수식)

They study <u>very</u> <u>hard</u>. 그들은 매우 열심히 공부한다. (다른 부사 수식)

<u>Luckily</u>, <u>I didn't lose my wallet</u>. 운이 좋게도, 나는 지갑은 잃어버리지 않았다. (문장 전체 수식)

■ 형용사와 형태가 같고 의미도 비슷한 부사는 다음과 같다.

early	late	hard	right	fast
(이른, 일찍)	(늦은, 늦게)	(어려운, 열심히)	(정확한, 정확히)	(빠른, 빠르게)
high	long	deep	low	near
(높은, 높게)	(긴, 길게)	(깊은, 깊게)	(낮은, 낮게)	(가까운, 가깝게)

■ 형태는 비슷하지만, 의미와 쓰임의 차이에 유의해야 할 어휘

late — lately	hard — hardly	near — nearly	high — highly
(늦게)　(최근에)	(열심히) (거의 ~않다)	(가까이)　(거의)	(높이)　(매우)

The library is very <u>near</u>. (가까운)　　　　　　　It's <u>nearly</u> seven o'clock. (거의)

Point 03 빈도부사는 조동사 be동사 뒤, 일반동사 앞에 쓰여요!

■ 빈도부사: 어떤 일이 얼마나 자주 일어나는지 횟수나 정도를 나타내는 부사이다.

■ 빈도부사의 위치: 대개 일반동사의 앞, be동사나 조동사의 뒤에 위치한다.
My father always watches that TV show. 우리 아빠는 항상 그 TV 프로그램을 본다.
He is often late for class. 그는 종종 수업에 늦는다.
You can always call me. 너는 언제든지 나에게 전화 걸어도 돼.

핵심만 콕! 문법 Check

A 괄호 안에서 알맞은 말을 고르시오.

1 They (strong, strongly) agreed with me.

2 Be (careful, carefully) not to drop it.

3 She studied (hard, hardly) for the test to get a good score.

4 They could (hard, hardly) believe his story.

B 〈보기〉에서 알맞은 한 단어를 골라 문장을 완성하시오.

> 보기
>
> sometimes   rarely   always   never   often

1 Our teacher is _____ late. (우리 선생님은 좀처럼 늦지 않으신다.)

2 She is _____ nice to everyone. (그녀는 항상 모두에게 친절하다.)

3 We _____ go to a Japanese restaurant. (우리는 자주 일식 레스토랑에 간다.)

4 My younger brother _____ goes to school by bike.
(내 남동생은 때때로 자전거로 등교한다.)

C 괄호 안의 단어를 적절한 위치에 넣어 문장을 다시 쓰시오.

1 I would like to drink something. (cold)

→ _____

2 We have information about the dinosaur. (little)

→ _____

D 우리말과 뜻이 같도록 괄호 안의 말을 바르게 배열하여 문장을 완성하시오.

1 나에게는 좋은 친구들이 많이 있습니다. (have, I, good, many, friends)

→ _____

2 그녀가 내게 뭔가 재미있는 것을 얘기해 주었다. (told, me, interesting, something, she)

→ _____

핵심만 쏙! 문법 Point

Point 04 원급 비교는 「~만큼 ~한」의 의미에요!

- **원급 비교**: 형용사/부사의 원급을 사용하여 비교하는 원급 비교는 「as + 형용사/부사 + as …」의 형태이고, '…만큼 ~한'의 뜻이다.
  She is as smart as Sally. 그녀는 Sally만큼 똑똑하다.
  He can run as fast as John. 그는 John만큼 빨리 달릴 수 있다.

- 「not + as/so + 형용사/부사 + as + …」는 '…만큼 ~하지 않는'의 뜻이다.
  She is not as tall as you are. 그녀는 너만큼 키가 크지 않다.
  Eric is not so funny as his younger brother. Eric은 그의 남동생만큼 재미있지 않다.

Point 05 비교급은 「-er」 또는 「more」, 최상급은 「-est」 또는 「most」를 붙여요!

- 형용사와 부사의 비교급은 대개 「원급-er」 또는 「more + 원급」이고, 최상급은 「원급-est」또는 「most + 원급」이다.

대부분의 경우	+ -er, -est	tall – taller – tallest
-e로 끝나는 경우	+ -r, -st	large – larger – largest
단모음 + 단자음으로 끝나는 경우	마지막 자음을 한번 더 쓰고 + -er, -est	big – bigger – biggest hot – hotter – hottest
대부분의 2음절 이상의 단어 형용사 + -ly 형태의 부사	more, most + 원급	beautiful – more beautiful - most beautiful quickly – more quickly – most quickly

- 비교급과 최상급이 불규칙하게 변하는 형용사와 부사도 있다.

good/well — better — best,   bad/ill — worse — worst
many/much — more — most,   little — less — least

A   다음 형용사/부사의 비교급과 최상급을 쓰시오.

1 quiet – _____ – _____   **2** noisy – _____ – _____

3 slow – _____ – _____   **4** fast – _____ – _____

5 fat – _____ – _____   **6** thin – _____ – _____

7 long – _____ – _____   **8** short – _____ – _____

9 many – _____ – _____   **10** little – _____ – _____

11 strong – _____ – _____   **12** weak – _____ – _____

13 big – _____ – _____   **14** small – _____ – _____

15 warm – _____ – _____   **16** cold – _____ – _____

17 easy – _____ – _____   **18** difficult – _____ – _____

19 cute – _____ – _____   **20** handsome – _____ – _____

21 wide – _____ – _____   **22** narrow – _____ – _____

23 bad – _____ – _____   **24** good – _____ – _____

25 hot – _____ – _____   **26** cool – _____ – _____

27 interesting – _____ – _____   **28** enjoyable – _____ – _____

29 funny – _____ – _____   **30** boring – _____ – _____

B   〈보기〉와 같이, 괄호 안의 단어를 활용하고 '원급 비교' 표현을 써서 다음을 한 문장으로 다시 쓰시오.

> ┌ 보기 ┐
> Mira reads 10 books a month. Sora reads 10 books a month, too. (many)
> → Sora reads as many books as Mira.

1 Paul is 170 centimeters tall. Andrew is 170 centimeters tall, too. (tall)
→ Andrew _____.

2 Tayeon sings well. Mia sings well just like her. (sing, well)
→ Mia _____.

핵심만 쏙! 문법 Point

Point 06 「비교급 + than」은 '~보다 ~한'의 뜻이에요!

- 비교급을 이용한 비교 표현은 「비교급 + than + …」으로 나타내고 '…보다 ~한'의 뜻이다.
  Yuna is stronger **than** you think. 유나는 네가 생각한 것보다 더 강하다.
  Minho runs faster **than** Minsu. 민호는 민수보다 더 빨리 달린다.

- 비교급 강조 부사: 비교급 앞에 **much, even, far, still, a lot**를 써서 '훨씬, 더욱'의 의미로
  비교급을 강조할 수 있다.
  She is much smarter **than** her friends. 그녀는 친구들보다 훨씬 더 똑똑하다.

  ※ very는 원급을 수식하는 표현이고, 비교급 수식에는 사용할 수 없다.

Point 07 「the + 최상급 + 명사 + in/of ~」에서 'in + 단수', 'of + 복수'의 형태로 쓰여요!

- 최상급은 셋 이상을 비교할 때 「the + 최상급 + 명사 + in + 단수/of + 복수~」의 형태로 쓴다.
  I am the prettiest daughter in my family. 나는 우리 집에서 제일 예쁜 딸이다.
  The middle room is the largest of all. 가운데 방이 가장 크다.

- 「one of the 최상급 + 복수명사」는 '가장 ~한 것들 중의 하나'라는 뜻이다.
  She is one of the smartest students in our school.
  그녀는 우리 학교에서 가장 똑똑한 학생들 중 한 명이다.

  ※「the + 서수 + 최상급」: Mina is the second tallest girl in our school. (몇 번째로 ~한)
  　　　　　　　　　　　　　　미나는 우리 학교에서 두 번째로 키가 큰 소녀이다.

  ※「the least + 원급」: Their stage was the least boring. (가장 ~하지 않은)
  　　　　　　　　　　　그들의 무대가 가장 지루하지 않았다.

Point 08 「비교급 and 비교급」은 '점점 더 ~한'의 의미에요!

- 「비교급 + and + 비교급」은 '점점 더 ~한'이라는 뜻으로 become, turn, grow 등의 동사와 함께 쓴다.
  His English ability gets better and better. 그의 영어 실력은 점점 더 나아진다.
  The weather is getting colder and colder. 날씨는 점점 더 추워지고 있다.

- 「the + 비교급, the + 비교급」: '~할수록 더욱 …하다'
  The more I get to know her, the more I like her. 그녀를 알게 될수록, 나는 그녀를 더 좋아한다.
  The more difficult the work is, the more interested he becomes.
  일이 더 어려울수록 그는 더 흥미를 가진다.

핵심만 콕! 문법 Check

A 괄호 안에서 어법상 알맞은 말을 골라 비교급 문장을 완성하시오.

1 I am (thin, thinner) than Yura.

2 Junsu sings much (better, well) than the other members of the choir.

3 Terry is a lot (intelligenter, more intelligent) than his friends.

4 I am (outgoinger, more outgoing) than my sister.

B 밑줄 친 부분을 어법에 맞게 고쳐 쓰시오. (단, 최상급으로 수정)

1 His drawing was <u>the better of</u> them all. → _____

2 This is <u>the taller tree</u> in this town. → _____

3 He speaks English <u>the better</u> of all of us. → _____

C 우리말과 뜻이 같도록 괄호 안의 단어를 활용하여 문장을 완성하시오.

1 저 책이 이 책보다 더 재미있다. (interesting)

→ That book is _____ _____ than this book.

2 개는 가장 친근한 동물들 중 하나이다. (friendly)

→ Dogs are one of the _____ _____.

D 우리말과 뜻이 같도록 괄호 안의 말을 바르게 배열하여 문장을 완성하시오.

1 날씨가 점점 더 따뜻해지고 있다. (warmer, and, the weather, getting, is, warmer)

→ _____

2 내 강아지는 점점 더 뚱뚱해지고 있다. (my puppy, becoming, is, and, fatter, fatter)

→ _____

3 책을 더 많이 읽을수록 우리는 더 많이 배운다. (the, more, we, read, books, more, the, learn, we)

→ _____

4 더 높이 올라갈수록 공기는 더 희박했다. (the, higher, climbed, we, thinner, the, air, was, the)

→ _____

01 짝지어진 두 단어의 관계가 <u>다른</u> 하나는?

① happy – happily
② slow – slowly
③ quick – quickly
④ easy – easily
⑤ near – nearly

02 [서술형]

우리말과 일치하도록 어법상 <u>틀린</u> 부분을 찾아 밑줄 긋고 바르게 고쳐 쓰시오.

> 그 연은 하늘 높이 올라갔습니다.
> → The kite flew highly in the sky.

→ _____

03 [서술형]

밑줄 친 부분을 어법에 맞게 고쳐 쓰시오.

> The weather was <u>perfect</u> fine.
> (날씨는 완벽하게 화창했다.)

→ _____

04 두 문장의 의미가 같도록 빈칸에 알맞은 것은?

> I am almost done with my homework.
> = I am _____ done with my homework.

① highly
② lately
③ nearly
④ hardly ever
⑤ early

05 우리말과 뜻이 같도록 빈칸에 알맞은 말을 <u>모두</u> 고르면?

> 부산에는 눈이 좀처럼 내리지 않는다.
> → It _____ snows in Busan.

① never
② always
③ often
④ rarely
⑤ hardly ever

[최다빈출]

06 어법상 옳은 문장을 <u>모두</u> 고르면?

① I usually go home late.
② She always is polite to others.
③ I rarely play computer games.
④ He never can do it alone.
⑤ We have often a chat.

[최다빈출]

07 형용사의 원급, 비교급, 최상급이 <u>잘못</u> 짝지어진 것은?

① difficult – more difficult – most difficult
② simple – simpler – simplest
③ good – better – best
④ little – less – least
⑤ late – later – last

08 빈칸에 알맞은 것은?

> This luggage is 10kg. That luggage is also 10kg.
> → This luggage is _____ that luggage.

① heavier than
② the heaviest
③ as heavy as
④ as heavier as
⑤ as heavily as

09 서술형

다음 대화가 자연스럽게 이어지도록 밑줄 친 부분을 어법에 맞게 고쳐 쓰시오.

> Paul: I am so excited about the soccer match tonight.
> Jane: You seem to really like soccer. Is watching soccer as enjoyable as playing soccer?
> Paul: No, I think playing soccer is <u>enjoyable</u> than watching it. Watching soccer is sometimes boring.

→ _____

10 밑줄 친 부분의 쓰임이 나머지와 다른 하나는?

① You are too <u>late</u>.
② I never wake up <u>late</u>.
③ I started to work too <u>late</u>.
④ Her class rarely finishes <u>late</u>.
⑤ Do you work until <u>late</u> at night?

11 〈보기〉의 밑줄 친 단어와 그 의미가 같은 것은?

> 보기
> The questions in the exam were <u>hard</u>.

① Mr. Kim works very <u>hard</u>.
② The idea is too <u>hard</u> for me.
③ You must study <u>hard</u> to pass the test.
④ Stones are usually <u>hard</u>.
⑤ Practice <u>hard</u> before the contest.

12 〈보기〉의 문장과 의미가 같은 문장을 모두 고르면?

> 보기
> Jay is not as tall as Teddy.

① Jay is taller than Teddy.
② Teddy is taller than Jay.
③ Teddy is shorter than Jay.
④ Jay is shorter than Teddy.
⑤ Teddy is not as tall as Jay.

신유형

13 빈칸에 알맞은 말이 나머지와 다른 하나는?

① I am older _____ my boyfriend.
② She walks much faster _____ I do.
③ This piano is more expensive _____ my piano.
④ They are smarter _____ other students.
⑤ The watch was as expensive _____ I thought.

14 서술형

괄호 안의 단어를 넣어 문장을 다시 쓰시오.

I will tell a lie again. (never)

→ _____

15 우리말을 영어로 바르게 옮긴 것은?

① 나는 너만큼 빨리 달리지 못해.
   → I can't run as fast as you can.
② 그는 우리 학교에서 두 번째로 큰 학생이다.
   → He is second tallest student in our school.
③ 날씨가 점점 더 추워지고 있다.
   → It is getting cold and cold.
④ 그는 우리 학교에서 가장 똑똑한 학생들 중 한 명이다.
   → He is one of the smartest student in our school.
⑤ 내 가방이 네 것보다 더 크다.
   → My bag is more larger than your bag.

고난도

16 어법상 옳은 문장으로 짝지어진 것은?

ⓐ He is the most strongest man.
ⓑ His condition got worse.
ⓒ I am not so smarter as he is.
ⓓ January is the coldest month of the year.
ⓔ Minsu is one of the most popular boy in school.

① ⓐ, ⓑ   ② ⓑ, ⓒ   ③ ⓒ, ⓓ
④ ⓑ, ⓓ   ⑤ ⓒ, ⓔ

17 서술형

괄호 안의 말을 이용하여 빈칸에 알맞은 말을 쓰시오

한국에서 아이스하키는 야구만큼 인기 있지는 않다. (popular)
= Ice hockey is not _____ _____
   _____ baseball in Korea.
= Baseball is _____ _____ than
   ice hockey in Korea.

18 다음 메뉴판에 대한 설명으로 틀린 것은?

menu	
Burger	$5.50
Ice cream	$3
Sandwich	$4.50
Fries	$2.50
Coke	$2

① A sandwich is cheaper than a burger.
② A burger is the most expensive of all.
③ Fries are not so expensive as a sandwich.
④ A coke is the least expensive of all.
⑤ Fries are less expensive than a coke.

[19~20] 대화를 읽고 물음에 답하시오.

A: May I help you?
B: Yes, please. I am looking for a gift for my mom.
A: Oh, I see. ⓐ Do you have special anything in mind?
B: Well, ⓑ she always wears a blouse, so ⓒ I want to buy her a nice one. ⓓ Would you show me something good?
A: Sure. How about this blouse?
   ㉠ 이것은 우리 가게에서 가장 인기 있는 블라우스에요.
B: Wow! ⓔ It looks great. How much is it?

19 밑줄 친 ⓐ~ⓔ 중에서 어법상 옳지 않은 것은?

① ⓐ   ② ⓑ   ③ ⓒ   ④ ⓓ   ⑤ ⓔ

20 밑줄 친 ㉠을 영어로 바르게 옮긴 것은?

① This is the popularist blouse in our shop.
② This is the more popular blouse in our shop.
③ This is most popular blouse in our shop.
④ This is the most popular blouse in our shop.
⑤ This is one of the most popular blouse in our shop.

21 서술형

괄호 안의 말을 재배열하여 문장을 완성하시오.

(1) 내 조카는 때때로 내게 편지를 써준다.
(a letter, writes, sometimes, me)

→ My nephew _____.

(2) 그의 편지는 점점 더 훌륭해지고 있다.
(his letters, better, and, better, getting, are)

→ _____

[22~23] 다음 표의 내용과 일치하도록 괄호 안의 단어를 활용하여 문장을 완성하시오.

Name	Height	Weight
Danny	170cm	65kg
Jay	165cm	65kg
Paul	175cm	70kg

22 서술형

A: Is Danny taller than Jay?
B: Yes, Danny is _____ _____
Jay. (tall) But Danny is _____
_____ Paul. (short)

23 서술형

A: Jay is the heaviest of all, isn't he?
B: No, Paul is _____ _____
of all. (heavy) Jay is _____
_____ as Danny. (heavy)

24 서술형

자신의 상황에 맞게 다음 질문에 완전한 영어 문장으로 답하시오. (단, 최상급 표현을 사용)

(1) Who is the youngest in your family?
(2) Who is the tallest in your family?

→ (1) _____
_____
_____

→ (2) _____
_____

고난도

25 서술형 심화

괄호 안의 단어를 활용하여 어법에 맞게 빈칸에 알맞은 말을 쓰시오.

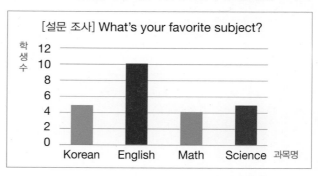

(1) _____ students like Korean than math. (many)
(2) Korean is _____ _____
_____ science. (popular)
(3) Math is _____ _____
popular subject in the class. (little)

CHAPTER 08

접속사와 전치사

접속사

접속사는 단어와 단어, 구와 구, 또는 절과 절을 연결해 주는 말이다. 접속사에는 문법적으로 대등한 관계의 말을 이어주는 **등위접속사**와 의미상 종속되어 있는 두 개의 절을 이어주는 **종속접속사**가 있다.

• 접속사의 쓰임

접속사	Anne is **smart** <u>and</u> **kind**.	(단어와 단어를 연결)
	Anne likes **learning new languages** <u>and</u> **doing volunteer work**.	(구와 구를 연결)
	We love Anne <u>because</u> she is the nicest girl in the school.	(절과 절을 연결)

• 구(phrase): '주어 + 동사'를 포함하지 않으면서 둘 이상의 단어가 모여 하나의 품사 역할을 하는 것
• 절(clause): '주어 + 동사'를 포함하고 있으며 둘 이상의 단어가 모여 문장의 일부를 이루는 것

전치사

전치사는 명사나 대명사 앞에 쓰여 장소, 방향, 시간 등을 나타내는 말이다. 전치사구는 문장에서 형용사나 부사의 역할을 한다.

• 전치사의 쓰임

전치사	I'll meet you **at the new library**.	(장소의 전치사)
	I'm going **to the new library**.	(방향의 전치사)
	Let's meet **at 8 o'clock**.	(시간의 전치사)

한눈에 쏙! 문법 Chart

접속사	등위접속사	and(그리고, ~와), but(그러나, 그런데), or(혹은, 또는)
	시간의 종속접속사	when(~할 때), while(~하는 동안에), before(~전에), after(~후에)
	이유의 종속접속사	because(~이기/했기 때문에)
	조건의 종속접속사	if(만일 ~라면)
	양보의 종속접속사	though, although, even though((비록) ~이지만, ~임에도 불구하고)
	명사절을 이끄는 종속접속사	that(~인/라는 것)
전치사	장소의 전치사	at(~에), in(~(안)에), on(~위에), over(~위에), under(~아래에), near(~가까이에)
	방향의 전치사	to(~에, ~으로), from(~로부터)
	시간의 전치사	at(~에 (구체적 시간/시점)), in(~에 (아침, 점심, 저녁, 월, 계절, 연도)), on(~에 (요일, 날짜, 특정일)), before(~전에), after(~후에), for+숫자(~동안 (구체적인 시간)), during+기간(~동안 (일정 기간)), by(~까지 (기한))
	구 전치사	in front of(~앞에), next to(~옆에), across from(~건너편에), between A and B(A와 B사이에), from A to B(A부터 B까지)

핵심만 쏙! 문법 Point

Point 01 대등한 것을 연결할 때는 등위접속사 and, but, or이 쓰여요!

- **and** (그리고, ~와): We were happy and excited.
  우리는 행복하고 신이 났다.
- **but** (그러나, 그런데): Jake is happy but Jane is sad.
  Jake는 행복하지만 Jane은 슬프다.
- **or** (혹은, 또는): Is the story true or false?
  그 이야기는 사실이야 거짓이야?

> *cf.* 'both A and B'는 'A와 B 둘 다'라는 뜻이다. 주어 자리에 올 경우, 복수 동사가 와야 한다.
> Both you and he *are* responsible for the accident. 너와 그 둘 다 그 사고에 책임이 있다.
> *cf.* 'either A or B'는 'A 혹은 B 둘 중 하나'라는 뜻이다. 주어 자리에 올 경우, B에 동사의 수를 일치시킨다.
> Either you or I *am* wrong.
> 너 또는 나, 둘 중에 한 명은 틀렸다.

Point 02 종속접속사는 시간, 이유, 조건, 양보를 나타내며, 명사절을 이끌어요!

1. 시간의 종속접속사: when, while, before, after + 주어 + 동사

- **when** (~할 때): Sandy was watching TV when her mom called her.
  Sandy는 그녀의 엄마가 전화했을 때 TV를 보고 있었다.
- **while** (~하는 동안에): My mom made a sandwich while I was doing my homework.
  내가 숙제를 하고 있던 동안에 엄마는 샌드위치를 만들었다.
- **before** (~전에): She has to go home before it rains. 그녀는 비가오기 전에 집에 가야 한다.
- **after** (~후에): The boy took a shower after he played soccer. 그 소년은 축구를 한 후에 샤워를 했다.

2. 이유/원인의 종속접속사: because + 주어 + 동사

- **because** (~이기/했기 때문에): I like winter because I like skiing.
  나는 스키 타는 것을 좋아하기 때문에 겨울을 좋아한다.

3. 조건의 종속접속사: if + 주어 + 동사

- **if** (만일 ~라면):
  You can stay here if you want to.
  네가 원하면 여기서 머물러도 좋아.

> ※ 조건을 나타내는 if절에서는 미래의 사실을 나타낼 때 현재시제로 쓴다.
> If the sun shines tomorrow, we will go on a picnic.
> 만일 내일 날씨가 맑다면, 우리는 소풍을 갈 것이다.

4. 양보의 종속접속사: though, although, even though ((비록) ~이지만, ~임에도 불구하고)

- **Though** they are rich, they don't waste money. 그들은 부자임에도 불구하고 돈을 낭비하지 않는다.
- **Although** it is December, it isn't freezing. 12월이긴 하지만, 엄청 춥지는 않다.
- **Even though** the project was hard, I did my best. 비록 과제는 어려웠지만, 나는 최선을 다했다.

5. 명사절을 이끄는 종속접속사: that + 주어 + 동사 (~인/~라는 것)

- 종속접속사 **that**이 문장에서 명사처럼 주어, 목적어, 보어로 쓰이면 명사절이라고 부른다.
- **that**절이 문장에서 주어로 쓰이면, 가주어 **it**을 먼저 쓴 후 진주어(진짜 내용을 말하는 주어) **that**절은 뒷 부분에 쓴다.
  That I got perfect score on the test is true. 내가 시험에서 만점을 받았다는 것은 사실이다.
  → It is true that I got perfect score on the test.
     가주어   진주어
- 접속사 **that**이 이끄는 절이 목적어로 쓰이면 접속사 **that**은 생략이 가능하다.
  I think (that) she is smart. 나는 그녀가 똑똑하다고 생각한다.
   주어 동사   목적어(절)
- 접속사 **that**이 이끄는 절이 보어로 쓰이면 앞에 나온 주어를 보충 설명 해준다.
  The problem is that I forgot to bring my wallet. 문제는 내가 지갑을 가져오는 걸 잊었다는 것이다.
              보어(절)

핵심만 콕! 문법 Check

A 괄호 안에서 알맞은 말을 고르시오.

1 John can speak English (and, but) Spanish well.
2 We should go home (before, while) it gets dark.
3 If it (rain, rains), I will stay at home.
4 If I win the lottery, I (buy, will buy) a new house.
5 (Even though, Because) the movie was over, people didn't leave their seats for ten minutes.

B 의미가 자연스럽게 통하도록 연결하시오.

1 If you wear this sweater,   •
2 If you eat vegetables,   •
3 If you hurry up,   •

• ⓐ you can stay healthy.
• ⓑ you can catch the train.
• ⓒ you can keep your body warm.

C 다음을 가주어 it으로 시작하는 문장으로 바꿔 쓰시오.

1 That Alison is funny is true.
→ _____

2 That we are planning Mom's surprise party is a secret.
→ _____

D 우리말과 같은 뜻이 되도록 괄호 안의 말을 이용하여 문장을 완성하시오.

1 비가 온 후에 하늘에 무지개가 뜬다. (in the sky, appears, after, it, rains)
→ A rainbow _____

2 그녀는 너무 더웠기 때문에 에어컨을 틀었다. (it, because, was, hot, too)
→ She turned on the air-conditioner _____.

3 부모님의 말씀을 듣지 않으면 후회할 것이다. (you, listen to, don't, parents, your, if)
→ _____, you will regret it.

4 Tom은 매우 가난하지만 행복하다. (Tom, though, is, poor, very)
→ _____, he is happy.

5 우리들은 언젠가 그가 성공할 것이라고 믿는다. (that, he, believe, will, we, one day, succeed)
→ _____

핵심만 쏙! 문법 Point

Point 03 at, in, on, over, under, near은 장소를 나타내요!

at	~에	비교적 좁은 장소, 행사, 각종 모임 등	at home, at the bus stop, at the party, at the concert
in	~(안)에	비교적 넓은 장소나 공간 내부, 도시, 국가, 하늘, 바다, 우주 등	in Seoul, in France, in the apartment, in the sky, in the sea, in space
on	~위에	접촉한 면의 위	on the table, on the ground, on the street, on 2nd Avenue
over	~위에	떨어져 있는 위	over the roof, over the rainbow, over the river
under	~아래에	떨어져 있는 아래	under the sea, under the tree, under the sofa
near	~가까이에	대상에 인접해 있는 상태	near here, near the bank, near the airport

Point 04 to, from은 방향을 나타내요!

- 방향의 전치사 to는 '~에', '~으로'라는 뜻으로 도착지나 목적지를 나타낼 때 사용된다.
  I went to Jeju-do last year. 나는 작년에 제주도에 갔었다.
- 방향의 전치사 from은 '~로부터'라는 뜻으로 원산지나 출발지를 나타낼 때 사용된다.
  He is from Germany. 그는 독일 출신이다.

Point 05 at, in, on, before, after, for, during, by는 시간을 나타내요!

- 전치사란 '명사나 대명사 앞(前)에 위치(置)하는 말'이라는 뜻이다. 대개 「전치사 + 명사(구)」의 형태로 문장에서 형용사 또는 부사 역할을 한다.

at	~에 (구체적 시간/시점)	at 3 o'clock, at noon, at that time
in	~에 (아침, 점심, 저녁, 월, 계절, 연도)	in the morning, in the afternoon, in the evening, in May, in spring, in 2030
on	~에 (요일, 날짜, 특정일)	on Sunday, on February 14th, on Christmas
before	~전에	before sunset, before lunch
after	~후에	after sunrise, after dinner
for + 숫자	~동안 (구체적인 시간)	for 3 days, for 5 months, for a year
during + 기간	~동안 (일정 기간)	during summer vacation, during the camp
by	~까지 (기한)	by noon, by Monday

Point 06 in front of, next to, across from, between A and B, from A to B를 구 전치사라고 해요!

in front of	~앞에	The church is in front of the clock tower. 교회는 시계탑 앞에 있다.
next to	~옆에	He is next to the Statue of the Liberty. 그는 자유의 여신상 옆에 있다.
across from	~ 건너편에	The boat is across from the ferry. 그 보트는 여객선 건너편에 있다.
between *A* and *B*	A와 B사이에	The post office is between the school and the market. 그 우체국은 학교와 시장 사이에 있다.
from *A* to *B*	A부터 B까지	She has to read the book from page 1 to page 30. 그녀는 1페이지부터 30페이지까지 읽어야 한다.

핵심만 콕! 문법 Check

A 괄호 안의 전치사가 들어갈 자리로 알맞은 곳을 고르시오.

1 I ① used to ② live ③ the U.S. (in)

2 We had ① fun ② the rock ③ concert. (at)

3 ① My school is ② 5th ③ Avenue. (on)

4 The picture frame is ① your ② head ③. (over)

B 〈보기〉에서 빈칸에 알맞은 말을 골라 문장을 완성하시오. (단, 한번씩만 사용)

> **보기**
>
> near   for   in   from

1 ABC은행은 우리 집 가까이에 있다.

→ The ABC Bank is _____ my house.

2 그 배우는 그 시점부터 유명해졌다.

→ The actor became popular _____ that time.

3 2020년에는 차들이 하늘을 날 것이다.

→ _____ 2020, cars will fly in the sky.

4 나는 서울에 10년 동안 살고 있다.

→ I have lived in Seoul _____ 10 years.

C 밑줄 친 부분에 유의하여 우리말로 해석하시오.

1 The boy ran away <u>from</u> the stranger.   → _____

2 They are going to go <u>to</u> the department store.   → _____

D 우리말과 뜻이 같도록 괄호 안의 말을 바르게 배열하여 문장을 완성하시오.

1 장갑은 코트 옆에 있다. (the coat, are, to, next, the gloves)

→ _____

2 눈사람은 집 앞에 있다. (is, a snowman, in, the house, of, front)

→ _____

3 은행은 학교 건너편에 있다. (is, the bank, school, across, the, from)

→ _____

4 풍차는 튤립과 장미 사이에 있다. (are, tulips, roses, between, and, the windmills)

→ _____

01 빈칸에 공통으로 알맞은 말은?

> • Many children went _____ the museum. There were many paintings and sculptures.
> • A guide gave pamphlets _____ the children and explained the area.

① for   ② to   ③ in
④ with   ⑤ at

[2~3] 빈칸에 알맞은 말이 순서대로 나열된 것을 고르시오.

02

> • Inho is handsome ⓐ _____ not nice.
> • Inho ⓑ _____ Mina are in the same classroom.

① and, or   ② or, but   ③ but, and
④ and, but   ⑤ or, and

03

> I'm planning to go to ⓐ _____ Canada or Australia ⓑ _____ summer vacation.

① both, at   ② both, or
③ neither, by   ④ either, under
⑤ either, during

최다빈출

04 밑줄 친 부분의 쓰임이 나머지 넷과 다른 하나는?

① I live in that house.
② She thinks that she is smart.
③ I know that he isn't from France.
④ Does he know that Minhee likes him?
⑤ My mom believes that I can be the best student.

05 밑줄 친 부분의 쓰임이 나머지 넷과 다른 하나는?

① When I have a cold, I drink lemon tea.
② Did she move to Busan when she was 5?
③ We cooked when we visited the elderly.
④ When she saw an old man fall down, she helped him.
⑤ When will you go to the Homeless Shelters?

06 그림과 일치하지 않는 문장은?

① A boy is in the bedroom.
② A boy is sleeping in the bed.
③ The bed is behind the drawers.
④ The drawers are next to the bed.
⑤ A panda doll is on the drawers.

07 밑줄 친 부분이 어법상 옳지 않은 것은?

① The train came on time.
② People left after the concert.
③ I usually wake up at 6 o'clock.
④ Ashley will arrive on the afternoon.
⑤ You'd better take an umbrella before it rains.

08 빈칸에 알맞은 말은?

I was so afraid that I couldn't sleep last night.
= I couldn't sleep last night _____ I was too afraid.

① and   ② but   ③ because
④ or   ⑤ when

09 어법상 옳은 것을 <u>모두</u> 고르면? (2개)

① He drinks milk on noon.
② She will go home if it will rain.
③ I did my volunteer work on a hospital.
④ I can make *kimchi* if my mom helps me.
⑤ If the vegetables are fresh, let's make a salad.

10 빈칸에 알맞은 말은?

비록 가끔 피곤하지만, 나는 자원봉사하는 것을 좋아한다.
→ _____ I sometimes feel tired, I like doing volunteer work.

① Although   ② But   ③ Yet
④ Even   ⑤ Because

11 밑줄 친 ⓐ~ⓔ에서 어법상 <u>틀린</u> 것의 개수는?

Tomorrow, Lisa will stay home ⓐ <u>alone</u>. She thinks ⓑ <u>what</u> she will have fun with her friends. She also believes ⓒ <u>that</u> everyone will come to her place and watch movies. She has called her friends, ⓓ <u>or</u> nobody answered. She ⓔ <u>will try</u> again later.

① 2개   ② 3개   ③ 4개
④ 5개   ⑤ 5개

12 〈보기〉의 밑줄 친 부분과 같은 용법으로 쓰인 것은?

┌─ 보기 ┐
The doctor told me <u>that</u> I have an eye problem.

① I like <u>that</u> car.
② Look at <u>that</u> girl over there!
③ <u>That</u> cartoon is not funny.
④ He thought <u>that</u> he got a good score.
⑤ We thought <u>that</u> picture was beautiful.

13 빈칸에 알맞은 말은?

The king was angry _____ the picture showed his bad side.

① because   ② and   ③ or
④ but   ⑤ if

14 빈칸 ⓐ, ⓑ, ⓒ에 알맞은 말이 순서대로 나열된 것은?

I am a violinist in the school band, so my violin is really important ⓐ _____ me. I have two expensive new violins, ⓑ _____ my inexpensive old one is my favorite. It is ⓒ _____ France.

① on, but, from   ② to, but, from
③ at, and, to   ④ to, but, on
⑤ to, or, from

15 서술형

우리말과 뜻이 같도록 괄호 안의 말을 사용하여 영작하시오.

나는 네가 훌륭한 요리사라고 생각한다.
(that, an excellent cook)

→ _____

16 서술형

우리말과 뜻이 같도록 문장을 완성하시오.

Q: Where should we meet?
A: 학교 앞에서 만나자.

→ Let's meet _____

17 서술형

우리말과 뜻이 같도록 주어진 단어를 배열하여 문장을 완성하시오.

나는 그가 내게 진실을 말했다고 믿는다.
(that, he, I, told, believe, me, the truth)

→ _____

18 서술형

다음 시간표와 내용이 일치하도록 빈칸에 알맞은 전치사를 쓰시오.

Tim's Timetable	
Period	Class
1	English
2	Social Science
3	P.E.
Lunch Break	
4	Music
5	Korean
6	Math

(1) Tim has Music class _____ the lunch break.

(2) Tim has English class _____ Social Science class.

19 서술형

빈칸에 공통으로 알맞은 한 단어를 쓰시오.

• _____ you try hard, you can make it.
• Please tell me _____ you can't answer the math problems.
• _____ I go to the playground, I will play soccer.

20 서술형

빈칸에 공통으로 알맞은 한 단어를 쓰고 우리말로 해석하시오.

(1) I think _____ Jisu is pretty.
(2) Jiho knows _____ his parents love him a lot.

→ 공통으로 알맞은 단어: _____

→ (1) _____

→ (2) _____

21 서술형

괄호 안의 말을 활용하여 영작하시오.

(1) 나는 밤 10시에 잠자리에 든다. (go to bed)

→ _____

(2) Sungho는 뉴질랜드 출신이다. (New Zealand)

→ _____

22 서술형

빈칸에 알맞은 말을 〈보기〉에서 골라 쓰시오. (단, 한 번씩만 쓰시오.)

> 보기
>
> from   to   at   in

Hello, everyone. This Thursday, we're going to go ⓐ _____ a museum. It is located ⓑ _____ Gwacheon. It takes about an hour to go ⓒ _____ school to the museum by bus. Let's meet at the main gate ⓓ _____ 8 o'clock. Don't be late!

23 서술형

밑줄 친 부분에 유의하여 영어 문장을 완성하시오.

(1) 고양이들이 <u>TV 앞에</u> 앉아 있다.

→ Cats are sitting _____

_____ .

(2) <u>소파 뒤에</u> 강아지 한 마리가 숨어 있다.

→ A puppy is hiding _____

_____ .

(3) 새들이 <u>하늘을</u> 날아가고 있다.

→ Birds are flying _____

_____ .

24 서술형

대화를 읽고 물음에 답하시오. (단, 완전한 문장으로 답하시오.)

Jinho: I had a soccer game this afternoon at Olympic Stadium.

Yumi: Did your team win?

Jinho: No. We lost. Our teamwork wasn't so good.

Yumi: I'm sorry to hear that. I thought your team was good at passing the ball and running fast.

Jinho: Not this time.

(1) Why does Jinho think they lost the game?

→ _____

(2) Where was the game held?

→ _____

25 서술형 심화

그림과 일치하도록 빈칸에 알맞은 말을 쓰시오.

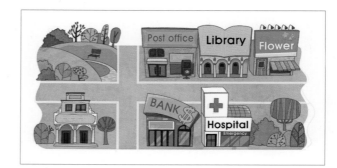

(1) The bank is _____ _____ the hospital.

(2) The hospital is _____ _____ the library.

(3) The library is _____ the post office _____ the flower shop.

A. 불규칙동사 변화표

B. 형용사/부사의 형태 변화

C. 혼동되는 어휘 정리

A. 불규칙동사 변화표

	원형	과거형	과거분사형	뜻
1	be	was/were	been	～이다, (～에) 있다
2	bear	bore	born	낳다, 참다, 견디다
3	become	became	become	되다
4	begin	began	begun	시작하다
5	bend	bent	bent	구부리다
6	break	broke	broken	깨다
7	bring	brought	brought	가져오다
8	build	built	built	짓다
9	buy	bought	bought	사다
10	cast	cast	cast	던지다
11	catch	caught	caught	잡다
12	choose	chose	chosen	선택하다
13	come	came	come	오다
14	cut	cut	cut	자르다
15	do	did	done	하다
16	draw	drew	drawn	그리다
17	drink	drank	drunk	마시다
18	drive	drove	driven	운전하다
19	eat	ate	eaten	먹다
20	feed	fed	fed	먹이를 주다
21	find	found	found	찾다, 발견하다
22	fit	fit	fit	맞추다
23	fly	flew	flown	날다
24	get	got	gotten/got	얻다, 시키다
25	give	gave	given	주다
26	go	went	gone	가다
27	have	had	had	가지다
28	hear	heard	heard	듣다
29	hit	hit	hit	치다, 때리다
30	hold	held	held	잡다

	원형	과거형	과거분사형	뜻
31	keep	kept	kept	유지하다
32	lead	led	led	이끌다
33	let	let	let	~하게 하다
34	lie	lay	lain	눕다, 놓여있다
35	lose	lost	lost	잃다
36	make	made	made	만들다
37	pay	paid	paid	지불하다
38	put	put	put	놓다, 두다
39	quit	quit	quit	그만두다
40	read	read	read	읽다
41	rise	rose	risen	오르다
42	run	ran	run	달리다
43	say	said	said	말하다
44	see	saw	seen	보다
45	sell	sold	sold	팔다
46	send	sent	sent	보내다
47	set	set	set	세우다
48	show	showed	shown/showed	보여주다
49	shut	shut	shut	닫다
50	sing	sang	sung	노래하다
51	sink	sank	sunk	가라앉다
52	speak	spoke	spoken	말하다
53	spend	spent	spent	(돈, 시간을) 쓰다
54	steal	stole	stolen	훔치다
55	take	took	taken	가져가다, 취하다
56	teach	taught	taught	가르치다
57	throw	threw	thrown	던지다
58	understand	understood	understood	이해하다
59	wear	wore	worn	입다
60	write	wrote	written	쓰다

B. 형용사/부사의 형태 변화

1. 대부분의 경우에는 규칙 변화

	원급	비교급	최상급	뜻
1	fast	faster	fastest	빠른
2	tall	taller	tallest	키가 큰
3	short	shorter	shortest	키가 작은, 짧은
4	long	longer	longest	긴
5	new	newer	newest	새로운

2. 단자음 + 단모음으로 끝나는 단어

	원급	비교급	최상급	뜻
1	big	bigger	biggest	큰
2	fat	fatter	fattest	뚱뚱한
3	hot	hotter	hottest	뜨거운
4	sad	sadder	saddest	슬픈
5	thin	thinner	thinnest	마른/얇은

3. 자음 + y로 끝나는 단어

	원급	비교급	최상급	뜻
1	busy	busier	busiest	바쁜
2	early	earlier	earliest	일찍/이른
3	easy	easier	easiest	쉬운
4	happy	happier	happiest	행복한
5	pretty	prettier	prettiest	예쁜

4. 2음절 이상의 형용사 대부분 / '형용사 + ly' 형태의 부사

	원급	비교급	최상급	뜻
1	beautiful	more beautiful	most beautiful	아름다운
2	difficult	more difficult	most difficult	어려운
3	famous	more famous	most famous	유명한
4	important	more important	most important	중요한
5	slowly	more slowly	most slowly	천천히

5. 불규칙 변화

	원급	비교급	최상급	뜻
1	good	better	best	좋은
2	well			(형) 건강한/(부) 잘
3	bad	worse	worst	나쁜
4	ill			병든, 나쁜
5	many/much	more	most	(수) 많은/(양) 많은
6	little	less	least	(양) 적은
7	old	older	oldest	나이 든, 오래 된
		elder	eldest	연상의
8	late	later	latest	늦은
		latter	last	나중의
9	far	farther	farthest	(거리) 먼
		further	furthest	(정도) 더욱

C. 혼동되는 어휘 정리

	어휘	품사	뜻		어휘	품사	뜻
1	close	형/부	가까운/가까이에	7	late	형/부	늦은/늦게
2	closely	부	면밀히	8	lately	부	최근에
3	hard	형/부	열심인, 딱딱한/열심히	9	near	형/부	가까운/가까이, 근처에
4	hardly	부	거의 ~않는	10	nearly	부	거의
5	high	형/부	높은/높게	11	most	형/부	최대의, 대부분의/가장
6	highly	부	매우	12	mostly	부	주로, 일반적으로

단기간에 마무리하는 8가지 핵심 비법

비법 담은 중학 영문법

법 은 학

Answer Key

영문법

1

특강편

단기간에 마무리하는 8가지 핵심 비법

비법 담은 중학 영문법

Answer Key

특강편 1

Chapter 01 일반동사

핵심만 콕! 문법 Check

Point 1, 2

A 1. like 2. look 3. writes
4. teaches 5. live

B 1. play 2. writes 3. has
4. studies 5. goes

C 1. wants 2. come 3. drinks
4. know 5. has

D 1. He, eats 2. enjoy, running
3. are, teach

Point 3, 4

A 1. don't 2. like 3. Do, don't
4. Does, doesn't 5. Do, I do

B 1. doesn't → don't
2. loves not → doesn't love
3. Does → Do
4. Do → Does, likes → like

C 1. don't eat 2. Do, work
3. doesn't write

D 1. doesn't grow 2. Do you help

내신 만점! 실전 기출

01. ⑤　　02. ④　　03. ⑤　　04. ③
05. No, he doesn't.
06. ④　　07. ③　　08. ①　　09. ⑤
10. does her homework before dinner.
11. The student doesn't study English every day. /
Does the student study English every day?
12. goes to bed
13. ③　　14. ②　　15. ②
16. Does Janet fold paper with them?
17. ③　　18. ②　　19. ④　　20. ③
21. ⑤　　22. ⑤　　23. ②
24. (1) Yes, he does. (2) No, they don't.
25. ① goes → go
② speak not → don't speak
③ write → writes

Chapter 02 명사와 관사

핵심만 콕! 문법 Check

Point 1-4

A 1. bike 2. leaves 3. knives 4. players

B 1. Mice 2. geese 3. fish 4. O

C 1. I drink two glasses of orange juice every day.
2. We need two bottles of water.
3. I want three pieces of cake.
4. She needs two loaves of bread.

D 1. are, customers
2. Are, coins
3. are, holidays
4. apples, are

Point 5-8

A 1. the 2. the 3. The 4. the

B 1. O 2. Autumn 3. O 4. by plane

C 1. the 2. a, the 3. the, the

D 1. the name of this tree
2. the ending of the story

내신 만점! 실전 기출

01. ④
02. Chris eats two bowls of rice.
03. ①, ②　　04. ①　　05. ②　　06. ①
07. ⓐ the Seoul → Seoul
ⓑ glasses → glass
08. ⑤　　09. ⑤
10. (1) two bottles of water
(2) a cup of tea
11. ③　　12. ③　　13. ②　　14. ⑤
15. ③　　16. ②
17. (1) pairs (2) piece
(3) slices/pieces (4) loaves, cups
18. two glasses of　　19. ①
20. ⓐ the ⓑ X ⓒ X
21. ⑤　　22. ④　　23. ①

24. There is, a small garden

25 (1) There is a glass of water.

(2) There are three pieces of cheese.

(3) There are two loaves of bread.

(4) There is an orange.

(5) There are three cups of coffee.

Chapter 03 대명사

핵심만 콕! 문법 Check

Point 1-3

A 1. that   2. these   3. This, mine
    4. these

B 1. This   2. That   3. those

C 1. It is windy outside. (비인칭 주어)
    2. It is very hot. (비인칭 주어)
    3. It is my middle school. (지시대명사)
    4. It is mine. (지시대명사)

D 1. Those books   2. It is
    3. It is raining   4. It is, hot

Point 4-6

A 1. one   2. ones   3. Any
    4. some   5. herself

B 1. a (new) hat   2. bag   3. boots

C 1. 나는 내 자신을 사랑한다.
    2. 그 소식 자체가 매우 흥미롭다.
    3. 너에 대해 이야기해줘.

D 1. books, borrow one
    2. socks, new ones, me
    3. any
    4. Some

내신 만점! 실전 기출

01. ①   **02.** ⑤   **03.** ③   **04.** ②

05. ones   **06.** ③

07. These are delicious oranges.

08. ④   **09.** ②

10. The winners of the contest are proud of themselves.

11. ③, ⑤   **12.** ③   **13.** herself

14. ④   **15.** ②

16. has some coins

17. any clean ones 또는 a clean one

18. ⑤   **19.** ③

20. [예시 답안] It's Monday [Tuesday, Wednesday, Thursday, Friday, Saturday, Sunday].

21. (1) It is sunny.   (2) It is cloudy and rainy.
    (3) It is 5 o'clock.

22. (1) These are   (2) This is   (3) That is

23. ③   **24.** ②, ⑤

25. (1) This   (2) themselves
    (3) Some   (4) myself
    (5) It   (6) any
    (7) one

Chapter 04 시제

핵심만 콕! 문법 Check

Point 1, 2

A 1. travels   2. helps   3. is sitting
    4. singing   5. isn't   6. doing, they are

B 1. is taking → takes   2. Does → Is
    3. Do → Are   4. is having → has

C 1. gets   2. is   3. is sleeping
    4. are making   5. is reading

D 1. knows   2. are you doing
    3. is running   4. starts

Point 3, 4

A 1. were   2. was   3. were   4. was

B 1. was   2. was   3. was   4. were

C 1. Yes, it was   2. Yes, I was
    3. No, they weren't

D 1. The game was not exciting.
    Was the game exciting?
  2. The questions were not difficult.
    Were the questions difficult?

Point 5, 6

A 1. cried   2. taught   3. tied
  4. stopped   5. stood   6. drove

B 1. go   2. Did
  3. didn't write   4. didn't go

C 1. visited   2. invited   3. dropped

D 1. Dennis went swimming yesterday.
  2. They had a good time last night.
  3. I spent time reading a book last weekend.

Point 7, 8

A 1. on Tuesdays   2. last night
  3. yesterday   4. ago
  5. these days

B 1. ⓐ reads, ⓑ was reading
  2. ⓐ is coming, ⓑ comes
  3. ⓐ study, ⓑ are studying
  4. ⓐ was playing, ⓑ played

C 1. rode   2. played   3. left   4. sat

D 1. Janet was looking for a key.
  2. Jessica is listening to music.
  3. They were singing and dancing.
  4. The boy was climbing the tree.
  5. The bird was flying in the sky.
  6. The old lady is sitting on a chair.

내신 만점! 실전 기출

01. ④   **02.** brought
03. ④   **04.** ②   **05.** ⑤   **06.** ①
07. ②   **08.** ③   **09.** ②
10. (o)pens, (c)loses
11. They aren't studying math now.
    Are they studying math now?
12. ④   **13.** ④   **14.** ②
15. Did you have fun?

16. (1) I was not(wasn't) good at science.
    (2) She did not(didn't) make a school newspaper.
17. ②   **18.** ③
19. She cleaned the living room.
20. She is listening to
21. The monkey broke a branch and held it
22. ④   **23.** ⓐ had ⓑ has   **24.** ④
25. (1) ⓑ picks → picked
    (2) ⓓ try → tried
    (3) ① buy → bought
    (4) ⓗ had → have

Chapter 05 문장의 형식

핵심만 콕! 문법 Check

Point 1, 2

A 1. happy   2. good
  3. unusual   4. nervous

B 1. bad   2. happy
  3. kind and gentle   4. beautiful

C 1. 바람이 부드럽게 불었다. (1형식)
  2. 우리 언니/누나/여동생은 고등학교에 다닌다. (1형식)
  3. Jay는 내 가장 친한 친구이다. (2형식)

D 1. My family lives in Seoul.
  2. His class is interesting.
  3. Alice became a doctor.

Point 3-5

A 1. 동사: bought   목적어: new glasses
  2. 동사: loves   목적어: us
  3. 동사: answered   목적어: his question

B 1. He gave us some tips.
  2. I can teach him English.

C 1. sent an email to
  2. made delicious sandwiches for
  3. asked many questions of

D 1. He asked some interesting questions of us.
  2. Jimin sent some books to her brother.

A 1. clean   2. fight   3. to carry   4. eat

B 1. My mom wouldn't let us play computer games.
   2. Mr. Johnson made us clean the hall.
   3. I had my son do his homework.

C 1. 나는 네가 항상 행복하길 원한다.
   2. 우리는 그가 제시간에 끝내는 것을 기대하지 않았다.
   3. 우리 엄마는 내게 설거지를 하라고 말씀하셨다.

D 1. He didn't let us come in.
   2. We saw them smiling.
   3. They heard me sing the song.

내신 만점! 실전 기출

01. ②   **02.** ⑤
03. Can you buy her a cake?
04. ⓒ. The apple pie smells delicious.
05. ③   **06.** ④   **07.** ①   **08.** ②
09. ①, ③
10. Her father looked healthy.
11. ⑤   **12.** ④
13. beautiful earrings to
14. ②   **15.** ③   **16.** ⑤
17. We should keep our desks clean.
18. I saw him cross/crossing the street.
19. ⑤   **20.** ⑤   **21.** ④
22. made them tired
23. My parents gave me a nice watch.
24. (c) to him → for him
    (e) come → to come
    (g) sent to me a text message → sent me a
       text message
    (j) let me playing → let me play
    (k) advised me read → advised me to read
25. (1) bought her a new, bought a new bag for her
    (2) wrote her, wrote a letter to her

Chapter 06 to부정사와 동명사

핵심만 콕! 문법 Check

Point 1, 2

A 1. to write   2. To swim
   3. to be   4. not to visit

B 1. to be   2. to watch
   3. not to wake up

C 1. where to go   2. what to choose
   3. how to use   4. when to stop

D 1. I didn't know where to hide it.
   2. tell me how to get to the library.

Point 3, 4

A 1. to visit   2. to sit on
   3. to meet   4. to write on
   5. to play   6. to live in

B 1. to finish   2. to tell
   3. to write with   4. to play with
   3. to play   4. to eat

C 1. anything to do
   2. time to go
   3. any good movies to watch

D 1. to become   2. to get

Point 5, 6

A 1. trying   2. Doing
   3. not passing   4. writing
   5. to buy   6. to enter

B 1. (a) 듣기 (동명사)
      (b) 듣고 있는 중인 (현재분사)
   2. (a) 춤추는 것 (동명사)
      (b) 춤추고 있는 중인 (현재분사)

C 1. Riding a bike is fun.
   2. Her hobby is playing the piano.
   3. We should(must) stop throwing garbage.

D 1. good at dancing
    2. enjoyed helping

Point 7, 8

A 1. swimming   2. playing

B 1. going   2. to return
    3. being   4. meeting

C 1. putting on   2. to smell
    3. fishing

D 1. What about studying
    2. spent the whole day solving
    3. decided to learn
    4. looking forward to watching
    5. Don't forget to bring

내신 만점! 실전 기출

01. ③   **02.** ④   **03.** ④   **04.** ①
05. It's not easy to get an A⁺.
06. ⑤   **07.** ③   **08.** ②
09. to play soccer
10. ⑤   **11.** ⑤   **12.** ①   **13.** ①
14. ②   **15.** ②   **16.** ②
17. how to use **18.** ②
19. Jina is going to go to Paris next week to see the Eiffel Tower.
20. (1) putting on (2) to buy
21. riding, playing[to play]
22. Don't[Do not] forget to set your alarm clock
23. The weather is good for playing sports.
24. What about calling
25. (1) showing → to show
    (2) learning → to learn
    (3) to play → playing

Chapter 07 형용사와 부사

핵심만 콕! 문법 Check

Point 1-3

A 1. strongly   2. careful
    3. hard   4. hardly

B 1. rarely   2. always
    3. often   4. sometimes

C 1. I would like to drink something cold.
    2. We have little information about the dinosaur. 또는 We have information about the little dinosaur.

D 1. I have many good friends.
    2. She told me something interesting.

Point 4, 5

A 1. quieter, quietest   2. noisier, noisiest
    3. slower, slowest   4. faster, fastest
    5. fatter, fattest   6. thinner, thinnest
    7. longer, longest   8. shorter, shortest
    9. more, most   10. less, least
    11. stronger, strongest   12. weaker, weakest
    13. bigger, biggest   14. smaller, smallest
    15. warmer, warmest   16. colder, coldest
    17. easier, easiest
    18. more difficult, most difficult
    19. cuter, cutest
    20. more handsome, most handsome
    21. wider, widest
    22. narrower, narrowest
    23. worse, worst   24. better, best
    25. hotter, hottest   26. cooler, coolest
    27. more interesting, most interesting
    28. more enjoyable, most enjoyable
    29. funnier, funniest
    30. more boring, most boring

B 1. is as tall as Paul
    2. sings as well as Tayeon

A 1. thinner   2. better
    3. more intelligent   4. more outgoing

B 1. the best of   2. the tallest tree
    3. the best

C 1. more interesting
    2. friendliest animals

D 1. The weather is getting warmer and warmer.
    2. My puppy is becoming fatter and fatter.
    3. The more books we read, the more we learn.
    4. The higher we climbed, the thinner the air was.

내신 만점! 실전 기출

01. ⑤   **02.** highly → high
03. perfectly   **04.** ③
05. ④, ⑤   **06.** ①, ③ **07.** ⑤   **08.** ③
09. more enjoyable   **10.** ①   **11.** ②
12. ②, ④   **13.** ⑤
14. I will never tell a lie again.
15. ①   **16.** ④
17. as[so] popular as, more popular
18. ⑤   **19.** ①   **20.** ④
21. (1) sometimes writes me a letter
    (2) His letters are getting better and better.
22. taller than, shorter than
23. the heaviest, as heavy
24. [예시 답안]
    (1) I am the youngest (person) in my family.
    (2) My father is the tallest (person) in my family.
25 (1) More   (2) as popular as
    (3) the least

Chapter 08 접속사와 전치사

핵심만 콕! 문법 Check

A 1. and   2. before   3. rains
    4. will buy   5. Even though

B 1. ©   2. ⓐ   3. ⓑ

C 1. It is true that Alison is funny.
    2. It is a secret that we are planning Mom's
      surprise party.

D 1. appears in the sky after it rains.
    2. because it was too hot
    3. If you don't listen to your parents
    4. Though Tom is very poor
    5. We believe that he will succeed one day.

A 1. ③   2. ②   3. ②   4. ①

B 1. near 2. from 3. in 4. for

C 1. 소년은 그 낯선 사람으로부터 달아났다.
    2. 그들은 그 백화점에 갈 것이다.

D 1. The gloves are next to the coat.
    2. A snowman is in front of the house.
    3. The bank is across from the school.
    4. The windmills are between tulips and roses.

내신 만점! 실전 기출

01. ②   **02.** ③   **03.** ⑤   **04.** ①
05. ⑤   **06.** ③   **07.** ④   **08.** ③
09. ④, ⑤ **10.** ①   **11.** ①   **12.** ④
13. ①   **14.** ②
15. I think that you are an excellent cook.
16. in front of the school.
17. I believe that he told me the truth.
18. (1) after, (2) before
19. If [if]
20. that, (1) 나는 Jisu가 예쁘다고 생각한다. (2) Jiho
    는 그의 부모님이 그를 많이 사랑한다는 것을 안다.

21. (1) I go to bed at 10 p.m.

(2) Sungho is[comes] from New Zealand.

22 ⓐ to,　　ⓑ in,　　ⓒ from,　　ⓓ at

23. (1) in front of the TV　(2) behind the sofa

(3) in the sky

24. (1) Because their teamwork wasn't so good.

(2) It was (held) at Olympic Stadium.

25. (1) next to　　　　(2) across from

(3) between, and

단기간에 마무리하는 **8가지 핵심 비법** 특강편